The Archetypal Cat

Sacred Egyptian cat

PATRICIA DALE-GREEN

The Archetypal Cat

with
illustrations

Spring Publications, Inc.
Dallas, Texas

To my husband

Originally published in 1963 under the title, *Cult of the Cat*, by Houghton Mifflin Company, Boston, and The Riverside Press, Cambridge, Library of Congress Catalog Card Number: 63-14209

Printed in the United States of America by Braun-Brumfield, Inc., Ann Arbor, Michigan
Published by Spring Publications, Inc., P. O. Box 222069, Dallas, Texas 75222

International distributors: Spring, Postfach, 8800 Thalwil, Switzerland
Also distributed by: Japan Spring Sha, Inc.; 31, Shichiku-Momonomoto-Cho; Kitaku, Kyoto, 603 Japan
And by: Element Books Ltd; The Old Brewery Tisbury Salisbury; Wiltshire SP3 6NH; England

Library of Congress Cataloging in Publication Data

Dale-Green, Patricia.
 The archetypal cat.

 Reprint. Originally published: Cult of the cat. Boston : Houghton Mifflin, 1963.
 Bibliography: p.
 Includes index.
 1. Cats—Folklore. 2. Cats—Mythology. 3. Cats—Religious aspects. 4. Cats—Psychology. I. Title.
 GR725.D29 1983   398'.369974428   83-833
 ISBN 0-88214-700-5

Cover drawing by Bradley A. Te Paske adapting John Tenniel's "Cheshire Cat" from his illustration in *Alice's Adventures in Wonderland* by Lewis Carroll.

CONTENTS

PART I

The White Cat

v

PART II

The Black Cat

PART III

The Medium

PART IV

The Symbol

ILLUSTRATIONS

ACKNOWLEDGEMENTS

It is impossible for me to acknowledge my debt to everyone whose advice and material have contributed to the completion of my work.

I do, however, feel that I am specially indebted to Mrs Rowena Phillips, whose material formed the nucleus of this book; and also to Mrs Neville Langton. The help so generously given to me by Mrs Langton has greatly enriched my work. She showed and discussed with me her wonderful collection of Egyptian bronze and faience cats, many of which are described in Part I of this book; and she allowed me to examine scrap-books containing notes and photographs collected by her late husband, who made a special study of the cult of the cat in Egypt.

I would also like to express my gratitude for the assistance I have received from the Staff of the Department of Egyptian Antiquities in the British Museum; and from Mr B. W. Robinson of the Victoria and Albert Museum.

The photographs for the Frontispiece and Plates *3, 9b, 10, 11, 13, 14a, 14b, 15, 17, 19, 22, 23, 24, 26, 27, 28* are the work of Jack Skeel, Orpington, Kent.

INTRODUCTION

There is one way in which cats differ from all other animals and that is in the effect they have on human beings.

Many people feel indifferent about dogs, horses or caged birds. They may have one of their own and be fond of it or they may not care for them at all, but either way they are not deeply affected. (A few are, of course, sentimental about their own pets, but one rarely hears of a dog, horse or budgerigar phobia.) Cats on the other hand produce strong human reactions, and there are comparatively few people who just "don't mind" cats. They seem to be strangely magnetic animals with an equally strong power to fascinate or repel, for most of us faced unexpectedly with one admit either that we "adore" cats or "can't stand the sight of" them.

We say, of course, that we love cats because they are good companions and useful mousers, or that we hate them because they kill or maim birds and are ungrateful or sly. But both these statements are rationalizations, for it is obvious that cats excite irrational feelings which emerge from a much deeper psychic level.

The cat has always stimulated people's imagination, attracting to itself a colourful and lively stream of myth, folklore, legend and fairy-tale. It has had fantastic powers attributed to it which have resulted in its being used in the secret rites of both white and black magicians. Cats have never been ignored; people have always felt *something* about them. In the past, either they were felt to be divine and were worshipped, or else they were considered demonic and were burnt.

Although in the East cats still play a part in religious ritual,

xiii

it is unlikely that anyone in the West worships cats, in a conscious and literal sense, these days. Nevertheless, black cats are still said to be lucky (or unlucky as the case may be); and many people betray signs of a cult of the cat, making these animals the centre of their lives, and treating them with a respect or dread that would seem appropriate only in relation to a supernatural being.

So the question arises: "What *is* it about cats?" We want to know precisely what the cat means to us all; where its power lies and why its image has survived for thousands of years in amulets, folklore and literature. No one seems to have got to the root of this, but I believe that the answer will be found if we make a thorough investigation of all that people have thought, felt, imagined and believed about cats, and are able to get some insight into the significance of it.

The mass of material that has come to hand seems to divide naturally into the light and dark aspects of the cat's nature and associations. And the titles of Part I and Part II of this book refer to the "whiteness" and "blackness" of the cat's reputation rather than to its natural colouring. (For instance a black cat may turn up in Part I if it is believed to have the power to heal sickness; and a light-coloured cat may be found in Part II if it was considered to be an omen of death. In Part III the colour of the cat is irrelevant.)

There is a Celtic belief that cats' eyes are windows through which human beings may explore an inner world. In examining the power that the cat has to raise our feelings and to stimulate our imagination we can hardly fail to learn more about human nature in the process.

In Part I we find awe-inspiring Egyptian cats receiving worship and sacrifice from human beings. We find cats bringing fertility to the fields of suppliant farmers, cats protecting the living and the dead from evil, and cats bringing

healing and happiness into people's lives. As the significance
of the beliefs behind these practices emerges it has much light
to throw on the feelings of those who "adore" cats.

Part II will strike a chord among *ailurophobes* – those who
do not merely dislike cats but experience hate, fear and
nausea in their presence. Here the feline demon comes into
its own with its blazing eyes and its monstrous fangs and claws.
The devil-cat emerges from the centre of the sexual orgies of
witches' Sabbats and of the ceremonies of black magicians.
Here the vampire-cat sucks the blood of sleeping men, and
the feline succubus drains their vitality.

Cat-lovers and cat-haters may find they come together
in Part III; for it seems that the cat has not only been thought
of as wholly good or evil, but has also been recognized as
forming a bridge between the two. This animal has the power
deeply to enrich our lives if, instead of obsessively loving or
hating the cat, we adopt a realistic attitude towards its
paradoxical nature, and allow it to communicate its wisdom.

"A world gone to the cats, every cat of the heart out . . ."
                                    TED HUGHES, "Of Cats"

PART I

The White Cat

MOST PEOPLE who readily admit that they "adore" cats would be shocked if you took them too literally. The cat has, however, a disdainful aloofness, a quality of meditativeness and inscrutability which has often been mistaken for divinity.

The Deity

The only fully-developed cult of the cat existed in Egypt and it lasted over two thousand years. No one knows when the Egyptian cat was first sanctified, and it was never officially considered to be divine. But such a distinction was too subtle for the general public, and Egyptian art provides ample evidence that the Egyptians treated these sacred animals as gods.

The bronze figure of a shaven Egyptian priest is to be seen (Plate *1*) kneeling in worship before a divine cat. The cat, which dwarfs the priest, is wearing necklaces; its ears are pierced for gold rings and its eyes were once inlaid with gold or jewels. It is a most impressive little group, and it emanates tranquillity.[1]

An engraving on a stone slab in the Turin Museum shows

[1] This, and most of the other Egyptian figures described in Part I, belong to Mrs Blanche Langton. They may be thought of as giving plastic expression to the many different facets of the nature of the cat-deity.

1

two men kneeling in adoration of a cat, while a painting on a cat-coffin in Cairo shows a holy cat sitting before an altar which is strewn with the sacrifices it has received. Amulets made in the form of little shrines are to be found with cats seated in them or, in some cases, on top of them. The Langton Collection includes a cartouche in the form of a seated faience cat inscribed with the name of King Shishak. (Shishak was the cat-worshipping pharaoh, referred to in the Old Testament, who ransacked Jerusalem during the reign of Rehoboam and carried off sinful Hebrews into slavery.)

The cat was considered very early on to be sacred to the Egyptian goddess Isis. It gradually came to be recognized as an incarnation of deity, and it was as the daughter of Isis and her husband, the sun-god Osiris, that the great cat-goddess Bastet (Bast or Pasht) emerged. Egyptian gods and goddesses have a confusing way of merging into one another, and it is important to remember this in considering myth and ritual with which Bastet is connected. For instance Osiris, Horus, Ra and Ptah were all different forms of the sun-god. Isis merged with Hathor, the cow-goddess, and with Mut, the Theban mother-goddess. Osiris, Bastet's father, was not only a sun-god but also a moon-god and god of the underworld; while Isis, her mother, was a sun-, moon- and earth-goddess. The worship of Bastet overlapped that of Isis, Hathor and Mut, and also that of the lion-goddesses, Tefnut and Sekhmet, according to the district and to which of Bastet's many aspects were being stressed. The cat-goddess had a solar son, Nefertem, by the sun-god, Amen-Ra, and Khensu, the lunar god, was her son by Ptah.

At the time when the Egyptian gods were taking form, the wild cat was venerated for its ferocity and rapacity – qualities which it shared with the lion. And Bastet was originally lion-headed, like the goddesses Tefnut of Heliopolis and Sekhmet of Memphis with whom she has so often been confused. Although it was in her later cat-headed form that Bastet became so immensely popular, she never ceased to be worshipped as a lion-headed deity, the two forms existing concomitantly through the last thousand years of Egyptian paganism.

The earliest known portrait of Bastet was found in a temple of the fifth dynasty (about 3000 B.C.). Here she is revealed as a lion-headed goddess who was honoured as "Bastet, Lady of Ankh-taui". One of the earliest pictures of a cat-headed Bastet is in a papyrus of the twenty-first dynasty, now exhibited in the Cairo Museum. The centre of the cult of the cat was at Bubastis, which was situated east of the Nile Delta. Consequently Bastet was known as the "Lady of the East" (Sekhmet bearing the title "Lady of the West"). Bastet was worshipped, among other goddesses, in the temple at Bubastis as early as the twelfth dynasty, but it was not until a thousand years later that this goddess really came into her own.

In the twenty-second dynasty (about 950 B.C.) Bastet took precedence over all other goddesses. She was known as "The Lady of Bubastis" and became an immense power in Egypt. King Osorkon II built a magnificent festival hall in Bubastis and dedicated it to Bastet. A relief found on the walls of the sanctuary showed the king endowing the goddess thus: "I give thee every land in obeisance, I give thee all power like Ra."

The temple of Bastet has been vividly described by the historian Herodotus, who travelled in Egypt about 450 B.C. It stood in the centre of the city of Bubastis and was virtually on an island, since it was surrounded (except at its entrance) by canals from the Nile, which were a hundred feet wide and overhung by trees. While the foundations of the surrounding houses had been raised, the temple remained on its original level so that the whole city commanded a view down into it. The temple was a splendid building in the form of a square, and was made of red granite. Stone walls carved with figures surrounded the sacred enclosure, which consisted of a grove of very tall trees within which was hidden a shrine. In the centre of the shrine was a statue of Bastet, the cat-goddess.

Little is known of what form the rites of the cat-goddess took. They probably included processions, litanies, antiphonal singing, invocations, revelations of sacred images and sacrifice. "Divine" cats were always to be found in the shrine of Bastet, for it was as this animal that the goddess was incarnated. Sacred cats kept in her temple were ritually fed, and those who tended them were exempt from liturgical services. The British Museum exhibits wooden figures of girls, carrying cats or kittens, who are thought to have been temple maidens.

One of the principal Egyptian festivals was that held in honour of Bastet. Herodotus stated that, of all the "solemn assemblies", by far the most important and popular was that annually celebrated at Bubastis. He described how, in April and May, thousands of men and women set off on the pilgrimage in parties which crowded into numerous boats. The voyage was gay if not positively orgiastic. Men played the flute, women a type of cymbal called crotala, and all joined in singing and hand-clapping. As they passed towns, the boats drew near to the banks and the women shouted bawdy jokes at those on the shore, often flinging their clothes up over their heads. This vulgar performance (presumably a form of ritual exhibitionism) was repeated at every town along the riverside and was a sign for those on land to start dancing.

When, eventually, the revellers arrived at Bubastis, they celebrated the festival of the cat-goddess, sacrificing many victims and consuming, we are told, vast quantities of wine. A military commander described how he "brought out Bastet in procession to her barge at her beautiful feast". This may be a reference to a rite known as the "coming forth", in which the statue of a deity left its own sanctuary and was carried in procession to pay a visit to another god. It was believed that a goddess (immanent in her statue) was, like human beings, entitled to pleasures and enjoyed a trip such as this. An inscription on a statue from Bubastis explains that the owner "made excellent monuments before her that she might appear to be pleased in all her festivals".

Such was the popularity of the cult of Bastet that images of cats (her animal incarnation) abound in Egypt. Cats have been portrayed in every conceivable activity, sculptured in every material from gold to mud, and in every size from colossal to minute. In Thebes a number of tomb-reliefs show cats beneath chairs. Particularly interesting is one depicting an orange-brown cat which has been tied to a chair-leg and is trying to get free. The chair is that of a deceased harbourmaster's wife who, sitting with her husband, is receiving offerings from river boatmen. Other reliefs show a ginger cat absorbed in eating a fish, a cat grasping a goose in its paws and a grey tabby with a long ringed tail just sitting.

A feature of the Ramesside period (about 1320 B.C.) was the satirical papyrus. These contained pictures of animals playing the parts of human beings, ostensibly displaying their weaknesses and vices. The British Museum has one, and here the cat is to be found driving geese, offering palm-branches to mice, and fighting against armies of rats.

It was during the Bubastite period (twenty-second dynasty) that the cat-cemeteries were laid out along the banks of the Nile. Digging in this area has produced bronze cat-effigies and a profusion of cat-amulets. The larger figures vary from peaceful, contemplative cats, dignified and awe-inspiring cats, to cats which have an ominous air about them. But all emanate vitality.

These bronze cats, which were made in temple workshops and sold at the stalls, were used as votive-offerings at shrines. It is considered probable that they were worshipped by many people, and recognized as symbols only by the elect.

Little amulet-figures of cats, pierced or ringed for suspension on necklaces, were found buried by their hundreds in cat-graves, and also behind walls and beneath floors of houses and temples.

They are carved in gold, silver, amethyst, jasper, cornelian, lapis lazuli, agate, quartz, marble, glass, stone and faience; and the mellowed glazes shift through brilliant blues, greens, yellows and soothing greys. They portray cats in every mood and position: there are meditative cats, alert cats, crouching, prowling, walking and pouncing cats, and cats who appear to be in full flight.

Although some of these cats are featherweight, others seem strangely heavy for wearing round the neck. Among the heaviest, and also the most charming of the amulets, are those consisting of cats on columns. The columns, perhaps three inches in height, are classic in form and usually made of faience. Often a single cat is poised majestically on high, but sometimes a couple of kittens snuggle together on the top.

Cats were used to decorate necklaces, rings, brooches and pins, and objects such as musical instruments and sceptres.

Although the cult of the cat was at its height during the twenty-second dynasty, it never dwindled during the next nine hundred years either in importance or in popularity. When, at the end of the Roman period, the image of the cat gradually faded, it did so, in company with those of all other animals, before the emerging image of Christ.

During the whole of Bastet's reign, household cats were treated with the greatest respect. Many of them were bejewelled, and they were allowed to eat from the same dishes as their owners. Sick cats were tended with solicitude, and stray cats were fed with bread soaked in milk and with fish caught in the Nile and chopped up for them.

A story is told of how a Persian army once won a victory over Egyptians by taking advantage of their reverence for cats. The Persians were besieging an Egyptian fort when their king had the brilliant idea of ordering his soldiers to throw live cats over the walls. The defending troops apparently allowed the city to be captured rather than risk injuring the animals they knew to be sacred and which they half-suspected to be divine.

The Sun

Cats certainly love basking in patches of sunlight. With his usual charm Topsell, the seventeenth-century naturalist, explained to us his conviction that: "The male cat doth vary his eyes with the sunne; for when the sun ariseth, the apple of his eye is long; towards noon it is round, and at the evening it cannot be seene at all, but the whole eye showeth alike." There are Chinese who believe that the size of the pupils of cats' eyes is determined by the height of the sun above the horizon, and lift up their lids to tell the time by them.

The cat-goddess, Bastet, was first worshipped as a form of the sun, which was the source and sustainer of life and light. Solar power belonged to the male principle and, although Bastet was conceived of as female, during the eighteenth dynasty she was often identified with her father who, in this case, was called not Osiris but Ra.

The Egyptians believed that, when the sun disappeared below the horizon every night, a combat of cosmic proportions took place in the underworld between Ra, the god of light, and Apep, the serpent of darkness. The battle was an eternal one for, although the sun rose every morning having overthrown the serpent and chopped him up into pieces, Apep was immortal and appeared with renewed avidity the following night.

The Egyptian *Book of the Dead* includes the Papyrus of Hunefer who was a royal scribe of the nineteenth dynasty. Plate *3*, a vignette from this papyrus, shows in the background a persea tree and in the foreground a cat with fiery eyes and bristling fur leaping on a spotted serpent and cutting off its head with a large knife. In another papyrus Ra, the sun-god, confirms our suspicions by asserting: "I am the Great Cat which fought hard by the Persea tree," and the serpent was, of course, the devouring Apep.

It was believed that, during a solar eclipse, a crucial battle was fought between the powers of light and darkness, and that the sun-god on whom the lives of the Egyptians depended was in the greatest possible danger. During this time mobs of people assembled in the streets shouting and shaking sistra (a kind of rattle) in an effort to spur on the celestial cat and to terrify the threatening serpent in their struggle beside the Tree of Life.

The central theme of great epic poems, and the most vital of all heroic engagements, is that in which a man enters into combat with a terrifying monster. The divine cat, in his nocturnal struggle with Apep, takes his place among the solar heroes of all mythologies in their fights with various forms of the Devil.

From the cat's identification with the sun has arisen "cat's-cradle", a name given to certain string-games. Games played by two people, in which string is wound in patterns round their fingers, are still played all over the world. People in a primitive cultural stage know a great variety of string-figures, many of which they use for purposes of sympathetic magic. The "cat's-cradle" is often employed to control the movements of the sun. Members of Congo tribes make cradles of string to encourage the sun to rest from its blazing activities. Eskimos try to entangle the solar cat, for they play their string-games after the summer solstice, hoping to hold the sun back from its long winter setting.

Egyptians thought of the sun and moon as the eyes of Horus, their sky-god. And although the power of the sun was of the masculine principle, the Egyptian word for "eye" was feminine. So Bastet, when she ceased to be identified with her father, was first worshipped as a lion-headed goddess who was described as the "flaming eye of the sun".

As a solar goddess Bastet was at her fiercest. She has been confused with Tefnut, the lion-headed goddess of the Old Kingdom who was known as the "Ethiopian Cat". Tefnut had migrated to Nubia, and she personified the cruel, searing heat of the equatorial sun; but Ra sent Thoth, the ape-god of wisdom, to bring her back to Egypt. A faience amulet from Bubastis shows the feet of an animal trampling on captives, and it is inscribed: "May Bastet give life and power".

This is not, however, the role usually played by Bastet, even in her lion-headed form, for she was a twin of Sekhmet of Memphis and, whereas both goddesses represented aspects of the sun, Bastet was always considered to be the milder of the two. Sekhmet, "the Great Cat", and Bastet, "the Little Cat", as they were known, were worshipped in the temple of the sun at Heliopolis. Texts speak of Sekhmet as a warlike goddess. She was the "Powerful" and the "Fiery One" who emitted flames against the enemies of the gods, for she incarnated the

fierce destructive heat of the desert sun. Bastet, on the other
hand, represented that life-giving warmth of the sun which
encouraged the growth of vegetation. A text referring to the
solar goddess runs: "Kindly is she as Bast, terrible is she as
Sekhmet."

When people wanted a fierce goddess to protect them they
called on Sekhmet; and when in need of gentler and more
personal help, they turned to Bastet. The Egyptian Trinity
was known by the composite name of Sekhmet-Bast-Ra.

When Bastet is lion-headed it is very difficult, in the absence
of inscriptions, to distinguish her from other lion-goddesses.
In coffin-paintings, on temple-walls and in papyri, the lion-
headed Bast is usually portrayed with a uraeus (or sacred asp)
rising from her head, and carrying in one hand a sceptre and
in the other an ankh. Occasionally she also bears a solar disk,
but this is more commonly worn by Sekhmet. The ankh, a
sign consisting of a T-shaped cross with a loop at the top, was
a symbol of life; the sceptre and uraeus were both emblems of
royalty, and the asps represented solar divinity.

At the British Museum there is a colossal sienite figure of
a lion-headed goddess who is crowned with a solar disk and
holds an ankh in her left hand. The statue is dedicated to a
priest-king of Upper Egypt who, the inscription states, was
"beloved by Pasht". There was also a statue, now unfortunately in pieces, of a cat-headed goddess with a head-
dress of sacred asps each of which was crowned by a sun. Little
faience figures of a lion-headed goddess, with a cat seated at
her feet, bring out the dual aspect of the sun-goddess.

In spite of the difficulties, however, Mr Neville Langton,
the Egyptologist who has made a special study of the cult of
Bastet, found that there were ways in which the lion-headed
Bastet could be distinguished from other leonine goddesses.
For instance, although the solar disk and uraeus worn together

are usually emblems of Sekhmet, when the uraeus-crown appears on its own it is invariably a sign that its wearer is Bastet. The enthroned sistrum-bearer is usually Bastet. Only Bastet and Thoth (the god of wisdom) are carriers of the sacred eye – about which more will be said later – and Bastet is often to be found wearing it in both her leonine and her cat forms. The scarab is a sign frequently engraved between the ears of both lion- and cat-headed bronzes of Bastet. This again distinguishes them from those of Sekhmet since, apart from Bastet, the only scarab-bearing deity is Ptah.

The scarab, or sacred beetle, was sometimes depicted in a boat, with its wings extended and holding the globe of the sun in its claws. It was believed that the scarab was self-produced. According to Egyptian folklore, when the male beetle wants to procreate, he searches for a piece of ox-dung which he shapes into a ball and rolls from east to west propelling it with his hind legs. Having dug a hole he then buries the ball, which varies from the size of a walnut to that of a man's fist, for twenty-eight days. On the twenty-ninth day the beetle throws the dung ball into water, from which its young soon emerge. It was believed that, as the balls of dung were rolled along the ground from east to west, so did the sun mount up in the sky, roll across it and then disappear below the horizon. As life came out of the ball of the dung-beetle, so all life sprang from, and depended on, the sun. From this it followed that the roller of the solar ball must be a beetle, and thus the scarab became a symbol (and even an incarnation) of solar deity.

The classical writer, Horapollo, maintained that there were three species of beetles and that one "has the form of a cat and is radiated, which, from supposed analogy, they have dedicated to the sun (the statue of the deity of Heliopolis having the form of a cat), and from its having thirty fingers corresponding to the thirty days of a solar month." The scarab, with which the cat was so closely associated, was, therefore, an emblem both of the self-begotten deity who created the universe, and also of the world which he created, since the maternal dung was shaped in the form of the globe.

Scarabs made of gold, ivory, faience, stone or wood were later inscribed with the names of kings, thus combining solar power with the power of royalty. A cat would be drawn on a scarab, and its image was sometimes combined with the name of Bastet. The bronze Egyptian sacred cat of the frontispiece shows very clearly the engraving of a scarab between its ears, and also of a winged beetle in the middle of its chest.

The solar Bastet could further be distinguished from Sekhmet by the fact that figures of the latter were often decorated with bracelets, armlets and anklets – an unknown experience for the lion-headed Bastet.

The Moon

The cat has always been associated with the moon. Like the moon it comes to life at night, escaping from humanity and wandering over housetops with its eyes beaming out through the darkness.

Ancient Greeks believed that at the beginning of the world the sun and moon created all the animals. The sun created the lion but it was the moon that brought forth the cat.

The life of the cat has been likened to that of the moon and in some cases even identified with it. Demetrius Phalarius, a Greek poet, claimed, for instance, that the cat's sympathy with the moon was such that the size of its body increased and decreased according to the waxing and waning of the lunar orb

Plutarch maintained that the cat had peculiar reproductory habits, producing litters consisting of first one, then two, then three kittens until it reached a litter of seven. Since, by that time, the total number of its young corresponded to the twenty-eight degrees of light which appear during the moon's revolution, the cat then stopped having kittens.

At Kirk Braddan in the Isle of Man there is a runic cross built into a wall near the south porch of the parish church. This is a wheel-cross, about four feet in diameter, and between each section is carved an animal. Of the four quadrants, three contain cats – one lean, one plumper and the third positively fat – while the fourth displays a shrew-mouse. (Although the common number of teeth in rodents is twenty-six, the shrew-mouse is said to have twenty-eight teeth, again coinciding with the days of the moon's revolution. This animal is fond of burying itself out of sight as the moon does at the end of its last quarter; and although it is not in fact blind it was believed by the Egyptians to be so.) The animals obviously represent the stages of the moon, and the cross is almost certainly a relic of moon- (and so of cat-) worship.

On the upper arm of the cross two cats supporting a human face between them are depicted. Plutarch informs us that "the human countenance between two cat-like figures upon a stone is designed to designate that the changes of the moon are regulated by wisdom and understanding".

Sometimes it was only the cat's eyes that were identified with the moon, changing as they do from the crescent to the round. Topsell described how "they shine more fully at the ful, and more dimly in the changing and wain". Plutarch explained that not only is the cat more active after sunset, but the dilation and contraction of its pupils are the waxing and waning of the moon.

So it would seem that the images of the cat and the moon

have been so confused that many people have been unable to distinguish between them.

The cat was worshipped by the Egyptians as a lunar, as well as a solar, goddess, and cats were held sacred in all moon temples. It will be remembered that both of Bastet's parents were moon-deities, and that her son, Khensu, was a moon-god. From one point of view Bastet was the moon-eye of the sky-god, Horus, and from another she was the night-eye of the sun-god, Ra. It was believed that when, during hours of darkness, the rays of the sun were invisible to man, they were mirrored in the phosphorescent eyes of the cat as the light of the sun is reflected in the moon.

Bast's name has been translated as "the Soul of Isis", and in later dynastic times the cat-goddess was very much involved in the cult of her divine mother. It has been suggested that the moon-cats of Kirk Braddan were a relic of Isiac ritual.

During the Greek period in Egypt, Bastet was identified with Artemis, the foreign moon-goddess. A myth tells how, when the Greek gods fled into Egypt hotly pursued by the monster Typhon, Artemis transformed herself into a cat and in this form took refuge in the moon. One Egyptian rock-temple dedicated to Bastet was called *Speos Artemidos*, the "Cave of Artemis".

We have seen how, as a goddess of the sun, Bastet could be lion- or cat-headed, but when she personified the moon she was always a cat. A lion-headed Bastet is easily confused with other goddesses, but a cat-headed deity is indisputably Bastet.

Sometimes Bastet has the limbs and tail of a cat, but she is typically depicted in bronze as an upright, cat-headed figure with human limbs and wearing a long, ribbed and heavily embroidered robe. Sometimes her robe is V-necked, and sometimes she wears a shawl over her shoulders. She may

1. Egyptian priest worshipping the cat *p. 1*

2. Mummied cat *p. 18*

wear a stiff, high collar made of beads or cowrie-shells fitting close up under her chin, or a pendant with a sacred eye engraved on it. An engaging bronze cat in the Metropolitan Museum of New York has a garland of lotus-blossoms in low relief suspended from a high, tight collar.

Bastet often has long pointed ears, but is also portrayed as bat-eared. The inner hairs of her ears are often shaped to represent the "feather of Maat" (Maat being the Egyptian goddess of truth), and the feather is then picked out in gold.

Bastet usually carries her three emblems – a sistrum, an aegis and a basket – and she is believed to be immanent in them. No other deity bears this trinity of emblems, which is unique to Bastet in her cat-headed form. (Leonine Bastets sometimes carry individual emblems but they seem never to have all three.)

Bastet is the only known Egyptian aegis-bearer, and she usually carries this little shield in her left hand holding it across her chest. Often the aegis is lion-headed, showing her close affinity to Sekhmet and reminding us that, in spite of her placid appearance, she can also be very fierce. Sometimes (as in Plate 8) the aegis has the head of a cat crowned with a solar disk and uraeus which are, of course, the emblems of Sekhmet.

The sistrum which Bastet carries in her raised right hand is often Hathor-headed, linking her with the cow-goddess of pleasure, and it usually has a sacred cat sitting either within the loop or on top of it.

When Bastet bears a rush basket, which she appears to use for carrying her kittens, it swings from the crook of her left elbow. Plate 8, a typical portrait of the goddess, shows her without her basket, but with four erect kittens at her feet.

Bastet is sometimes portrayed as slim and elegant, some-times as staid and statuesque. In some moods she is alert and vibrant, in others rather more restful. But all the still silent images of the goddess have a dignity about them – one is always aware of a stately presence.

One rare and particularly interesting little bronze in the Langton Collection shows Bastet dressed in a short, wide ribbed robe hardly covering her knees, and holding a kitten in her right hand exactly as if it were a sistrum. The collection also includes two dark-green faience baskets such as the goddess carries on her arm, and a third with a seated kitten hidden inside it, confirming our conjecture as to its use. Finally, we find the "holy one", complete with embroidered robe, aegis, sistrum and basket, emerging from a turreted shrine. This is a most impressive little image with the quality of a revelation.

The Immortal

The cat that is shown (on the stele in the Turin Museum) being worshipped by two devotees is described in an accompanying text as "the beautiful cat which *endures, endures*". When a cat curls up with its head touching its tail, it forms a circle and as such is a symbol of eternity. The circle has no beginning or end; in its roundness there is no before or after. It is static, resting in itself, perfect and complete.

In Scotland, single standing stones of the Neolithic age are often known as "cat stanes"; and near Maidstone, in Kent, there is a famous cromlech, consisting of a vast block of sandstone resting on three other blocks, which is known as Kit's Coty House. No one knows why such ancient monuments should be associated with cats, but they are symbols of indestructibility and perpetuity.

The cat is a strong, hardy animal. It is suspicious and

cautious in its approach to other creatures, and in its wild state it is ferocious. If it falls from a height it miraculously lands on its feet which are exceptionally well padded so that it can do so without injury. If not actually immortal the cat is at least reputed to have nine lives.

Nine is a mystical number, composed as it is of a trinity of trinities, and from the earliest times it has been regarded as specially significant. The River Styx encompassed the Greek hell in nine circles; in Teutonic mythology there were nine worlds over which Odin gave power to Freya, the goddess of love. According to an Egyptian system of astronomy there were nine spheres, and the Egyptian pantheon consisted of three companies of nine gods. The Greek Apollo (brother of the moon-goddess, Artemis, with whom Bastet was identified) created the lunar year which consisted of nine months; and in Christian myth the fateful hour of Christ's death was the ninth.

It is said that if you take even one of a cat's nine lives it will haunt you and work its vengeance on you. In Europe, and also in Africa, to kill or even maltreat a cat was believed to bring bad luck. In India, where Parsees respected the cat as an uncanny animal, the destruction of one was treated as a serious crime. But only in Egypt was cat-murder punished by the death penalty, and Herodotus has described how a Roman soldier who killed a cat was promptly lynched by a crowd of outraged Egyptians.

When a household cat died in Egypt, members of the family shaved their eyebrows as a sign of mourning. The cat's master placed the body in a linen sheet, and carried it amidst the bitter lamentations of the bereaved to a sacred house where it was treated with drugs and spices by an embalmer. It was then laid in a specially prepared case and was finally deposited in sacred vaults. Food was often buried with the cats, and it was believed that this food was continually renewed by incantations recited by priests. In a tomb at Abydos containing the skeletons of seventeen cats, rows of tiny offering-pots were found in a recess presumably for receiving milk.

Cat-funerals were accompanied by much breast-beating, by wine-drinking and the clashing of cymbals. Cats which, during their lifetime, had served in temples and been worshipped as representatives of Bastet, were buried in a more sumptuous manner than others and treated with additional honours. The expenses connected with cat-funeral rites were met by the donations of pious individuals. Embalmed cats were dispatched in thousands from all parts of Egypt to Bubastis, where they were ranged on shelves of collective tombs in an immense cemetery devoted to them.

Plate 2 shows an elegant cat-mummy which was found in a tomb at Abydos. It is a typical example of a rich man's mummied cat. The linen bandages are dyed in two colours and are elaborately wound and plaited to form beautiful patterns. The head is encased in papier-mâché, with painted linen discs sewn on to represent eyes and nostrils. Midribs of palm-leaves are used to imitate ears, which are always very carefully pricked up. A poor man's cat would be rolled up in a simple bundle, but the rolling was carefully and respectfully carried out.

The honoured relics of cats were also enclosed in mummy-cases. The case, which was anything up to three feet high, consisted of wood or of coloured, plaited straw which was hollowed out in the shape of a standing or seated cat. It was surmounted by a painted, wooden cat's head. Bodies or bones of cats or kittens were enclosed in smaller bronze or faience cat-figures. Mummy-cases sometimes had eyes formed of crystal inlaid with gold, the pupils being of black obsidian.

Then there was the little, bronze cat-coffin, which often had the figure of a cat perched on its lid. The Langton Collection includes a particularly charming one which is three inches in length and so suitable only for a new-born kitten or for a foetus. It is guarded by four bronze kittens sitting on their haunches on its lid.

Embalmment was based on belief in the cat's immortality, for it was hoped that if the physical body was kept alive the soul of the animal might return. The cat was closely associated with the idea of resurrection, and the next section will refer to the part it played in the mummification ceremonies of human beings. Cat-priests have been portrayed taking part in rites connected with life beyond the tomb.

The ankh which the solar Bastet sometimes carried is a symbol of eternity. The word ankh means life – the life, presumably, of the sun since its loop represented a solar disk. Not only did the living wear the ankh as an amulet to prolong their lives, but the emblem was also buried with the dead to renew life and effect resurrection. The scarab was the other sun-symbol with which the cat was closely associated, and scarabs were also buried with the dead to give them the power to rise again. (A scarab-shaped spot is not an uncommon marking to be found between cats' ears, and it has been thought probable that such markings were responsible for the recognition of the divinity of those Egyptian cats selected for temple life.)

Cats have been believed to enshrine spirits of the dead. Members of certain Gold Coast tribes are still convinced that when people die their souls pass into cats. In Japan a black patch on the back of a cat (supposed to represent a woman in a kimono) is looked upon as a "sacred mark" by certain sects. All such cats are sent to a temple, for it is assumed that they contain the souls of ancestors.

The "temple-mark" of the Siamese cat is a shadowy patch low down on the back of its neck. It is said that a god once picked up a sacred Siamese cat and left the shadow of his hands for ever on its descendants. At one time, when a member of Siamese royalty died one of his cats would be buried alive with him. The tomb had small holes pierced in the roof, and when the cat succeeded in escaping through one of these the priests knew that the soul of the prince had passed into the cat and they conducted the animal to the temple with appropriate honours. When the young King of Siam was crowned in 1926, a white cat was carried by court chamberlains in the procession to the throne-room. Presumably this was the cat which carried the soul of the deceased monarch.

The temple-cats of Siam take part in religious ritual. Members of the black-coated, golden-eyed variety are to be found reclining on cushions in richly ornamented cages. They have also been seen in gilded cages with incense burning before them, and offerings of food at their sides.

In the eighteenth century cats played an important part in the ceremonies of a religious order residing in North Burma. The priests practised secret rites in a subterranean temple called *Lao-Tsun*, "The Abode of the Gods". They kept a hundred sacred Burmese cats, and one, a golden-eyed cat called Sinh, sat with his master at the foot of the statue of a goddess who had eyes of sapphire and presided over the transmutation of souls. Sinh's master was an aged, golden-bearded high priest, who lived in rapt contemplation of the goddess. According to legend, when the high priest died one night, Sinh immediately leapt onto his master's throne, taking up his position facing the goddess. For seven days this sacred cat, bearing the soul of the high priest, refused all food and continued to stand erect, gazing into the sapphire eyes of the goddess.

When the time came for Sinh's master to be replaced, the priests assembled, and a hundred temple-cats appeared walking in slow procession. The priests prostrated themselves and waited until the cats, which, they believed, enshrined the souls of their elders, had surrounded their chosen successor to the high priest.

The spirituality of the cat was emphasized when, in later Egyptian theology, Bastet was represented as having wings. It was in the form of a sparrow-hawk that her mother, Isis, had hovered over the dead body of Osiris, causing his breath to return by the fanning of her wings. Mut, the Theban mother-goddess, was often depicted with the head of a vulture. So it was probably when she was identified with one of the mother-goddesses that Bastet was represented as a cat-headed hawk, and was a symbol of the soaring immortal soul.

The Seer

The eyes of cats are probably responsible for much of the spirituality and the magic that have been attributed to these animals. The cat shares with the snake an unblinking gaze, and its disconcerting habit of staring fixedly into human eyes has a compelling power which affects some people deeply. The pupils of their eyes shine in the darkness, and in half-light some reflect a fiery glow.

The Egyptian name for the cat is *mau*, which means "to see". As we know, cats' eyes have been intimately linked with movements of the sun and moon; and it was because Bastet represented the eyes of the all-seeing Horus that she was worshipped as both a solar and a lunar goddess.

According to Egyptian myth the original sky-god had only one eye, and when he wept it was from the tears of this eye that the human beings who peopled the earth were created. This primordial eye was detachable, and the creator-god, whose two children had been separated from him, sent the eye off into the abyss to search for his wandering offspring. The eye found the children, but when it returned it was to discover that another eye had grown and had usurped its place in the god's face.

In order to pacify the outraged eye, the creator-god transformed it into a cobra and elevated it to a position on his forehead, from which it thenceforth guarded his crown. This rearing, poisonous snake which encircled the god's brow was given great majesty, power and magic; but the eye could never be fully or permanently appeased and the anger of the eye (or the aggression of the snake) was no doubt an expression of the raging heat of the sun.

The eye that had ousted the "elevated" one was probably the milder sun, and these two eyes later developed into the solar goddesses, Sekhmet and Bastet, the lion and the cat.

Again we find the snake and cat closely connected, for when the sky-god became known as Horus it was as if the light of the single eye of the creator had been split into two – the light of the sun and the light of the moon. And the power that had first been known as the cobra came to be thought of as the solar and lunar cat.

There is also the myth of the moon, which tells how Horus temporarily lost his lunar eye. The sky-god once engaged in a blood-curdling combat with the Egyptian devil whose name was Set. During the struggle, in which Horus seized Set's testicles, the devil tore the left eye out of the sky-god's head and flung it over the edge of the world. Luckily, Thoth, the ape-god of wisdom who was also guardian of the moon, saw what had happened and went off into the outer darkness to search for it. He eventually found the lunar orb lying broken in pieces; and these he gathered up and re-assembled, restoring the full moon to Horus. Another version of the myth says that when Set tore out the moon-eye he swallowed it, but Ra insisted that he put it back where it belonged.

The relief on the wall of the temple at Bubastis showed that, when King Osorkon first endowed Bastet with power, he offered to her an amulet of the "sacred eye". These eyes of Horus, which the cat-goddess represented, had a very powerful magic of their own (perhaps inherited from the archaic cobra). The name for the sacred eye is utchat, a word meaning "to be in good mental and physical health", and the right or solar eye of Horus was considered to be the source of all human health and happiness.

Many cat-amulets have the utchat engraved on them and cats with sacred eyes were often depicted on scarabs, the eye giving the object its power of protection. Utchats frequently adorn the larger bronze figures of cats, having either been engraved directly on their chests or on a suspended pendant carved in relief (see frontispiece).

Where the utchat is itself used as an amulet, it is usually made as a solid plaque. Sometimes a solar disk and uraeus were added to the sacred eye; sometimes it was provided with the wing, leg and claw of a bird, presumably to emphasize its spirituality. Plate 6b shows such an utchat amulet which in this case consists of a large eye with a secondary one inset above it; nineteen long-eared cats sitting on their haunches in rows fill the space above and below the pupil. Separately, the images of the cat and the eye are powerfully magical, and here, in conjunction, the two enhance the magic of one another. Since Bastet was the "flaming eye of Horus" there is a sense in which the "sacred eye" is always that of the cat.

The eyes of Horus protected not only the living but also the dead, and in the sixth dynasty twin utchats appeared on coffins, indicating that the deceased were under the protection of solar and lunar deities.

To be cat-eyed is to be able to see in the dark, and the cat-goddess, as a personification of the moon and as daughter of Osiris, god of the dead, had her part to play in the underworld. An amulet has been found bearing the inscription: "May Bastet revivify the deceased among the glorified." A vignette in a funerary papyrus shows a cat sitting on its haunches, with a scarab beetle depicted above it, and below it a rectangle containing a sacred eye. This cat (see Plate 5) was believed to take part in the mummification rites of human beings, and was known as "The Cat of Lapis Lazuli". (Utchats were often carved from lapis lazuli – perhaps because its intense blue speckled with gold seemed specially suitable for the eye of a sky-god.)

The ceremonies connected with mummification were magical in origin. As each bandage was laid in position, words were uttered which had the power to preserve the part swathed. After consecration and an invocation to the deceased, the priest took a vase containing ten perfumes and smeared the body twice from head to foot. Certain precious stones were laid on the mummy, and these were considered to have magical significance – cornelian, it was said, strengthened the dead man's steps, and crystal lighted his face. A special anointing preceded the bandaging of the head; then the mummy's left hand was filled with the thirty-six substances which were used in embalming and symbolized the thirty-six forms in which the god Osiris revealed himself. When the anointing and bandaging were finally complete the ceremony closed with an appropriate address to the participants.

The text of a funerary papyrus, such as the one containing "The Cat of Lapis Lazuli", was concerned with the welfare of the dead. The utchat drawn near the Cat of Lapis Lazuli emphasized her power to give protection against evil unseen in the darkness by human beings. Deities were believed to be immanent in their pictorial representations, and such was the power of the word that the written formulae accompanying them were capable of determining their actions. If, therefore, the Cat of Lapis Lazuli can be taken to represent Bastet, references in the papyrus to the fact that she took part in mummification rites would actually have effected the deity's participation in them. As we know, the purpose of embalmment was to ensure that the body lived for ever, and the scarab stressed the cat's association with resurrection.

The cat's reputation for second sight sometimes resulted in its suffering terrible tortures at the hands of people who wanted to acquire the faculty themselves. (An account of such practices will be given in the section on the cat *qua* victim.) The eyes of a black cat mixed with the gall of a man was a charm designed to endow human beings with second sight. Those who coveted the power to see demons could find the following prescription in the Jewish Talmud: "Find and burn the placenta of the first litter of a black cat [which must have been one of its mother's first litter], then beat it to a powder and rub it into the eyes." It was not, however, always considered necessary to kill a cat in order to participate in its occult powers. Its reputation was such that people in England used to believe that the mere proximity of a tortoise-shell cat helped one to develop powers of clairvoyance, and children were encouraged to play with them for this reason.

The cat-goddess of the moon lit up the night, throwing light on things which would otherwise be concealed. By the light of the sun we see the outer world, but the moon lights up a world hidden in darkness and it is the cat-goddess who brings us *in*-sight with her illumination of the "under", or "inner", world. The moon may be thought of as a searcher – a seeker of the truth. Bastet was often known as the "Lady of Truth", and a scarab engraved with a cat is inscribed, "Bastet is truth". The beams of the moon point out the way – the *Tao*; and a narrow path or bridge is called a "cat-walk", perhaps because the cat-goddess chooses the precarious Middle Way. In French folklore the black cat can show men the way to wealth, for peasants will tell you that, if you tie a black cat to a spot where five roads meet and then let it loose, it will lead you straight to hidden treasure.

It is probably because it was believed that the light of the sun and moon shines through its eyes that the cat came to be associated with Christianity, for Christ is the "Light of the World". Although the game known as "cat's-cradle" had an ancient solar derivation, the name was later interpreted by Christians as "cratch-cradle" – the manger (*crèche*) in which Christ was laid. Christ was mythologically linked with dying and resurrecting sun-gods, and there is an Italian legend that, at the moment when Jesus was born in the stable, a cat gave birth to a kitten under the manger.

The Healer

A healer is, from one point of view, someone who rids us of poison. Cats do their best to keep our lives free from poisonous influences in so far as these are represented by the venomous snake. (Some people believe that if a house is deserted by cats there will always be illness in it.) In Paraguay cats are used for snake-hunting and some have been known to struggle with rattlesnakes for hours. They are very adept in their method of dealing with these reptiles, striking them with a paw then slipping to one side to avoid the counterattack. It has been suggested that the reason cats were considered holy by the Egyptians was that they could be relied on to destroy venomous snakes. We have seen how the serpent, a symbol of cosmic evil in ancient Egypt, was overcome at the eclipse by the solar cat.

Bastet, the cat-goddess, had the power to heal; and there is a scarab engraved with a cat inscribed "Bastet, the Nurse". (Again we find the cat and snake sharing their respective attributes, for the latter has always been used as a symbol of healing. In spite of the fact that in a certain context the snake is a healer, however, it also represents its opposite: the disease. And when Bastet or her feline representative is found attacking a snake, the snake expresses all that is poisonous, and all that terrifies and revolts us most.)

The cat's reputation for killing snakes extended to one for healing those bitten by them, and Bastet was believed to be specially successful in her treatment of people or animals suffering from poisonous bites or stings. There is a myth which tells how she was herself once stung by a scorpion and saved from death only by the first-aid she received from Ra.

This story was engraved on a slab of stone (in about 370 B.C.) now known as the Metternich Stele (Plate 6a) and exhibited in the Metropolitan Museum of New York. The stele is covered with magical texts, one of which is labelled "Spell for exorcising poison from a cat". The spell, which consisted of reciting the drama of Bastet, was used on behalf of household or temple-cats which had been stung by scorpions, and it was believed that by identifying the sick cat with Bastet it would share in the healing that the goddess had received.

According to the text Bastet cried out to her father for help:

"O Ra, come to your daughter whom the scorpion has

stung on a lonely road. Her cries reach heaven. The poison which has entered her limbs flows through her veins. She has sucked the wound but, lo, the poison is in her limbs. Come then with your might, with your frightfulness, with your magnificence."

Ra then replies that he is protecting her and will overthrow the poison. An incantation follows in which each limb of the cat is mentioned individually and placed under the protection of a different god. A tourniquet is then applied inscribed with the further spell: "O evil poison which is in every limb of this sick cat, come forth on earth."

On the base of the stele there is a short spell for a sick cat addressed to Bastet.

The Metternich stele was one of those known as the Cippi of Horus and it was used as a household talisman. On it was carved the figure of Horus, Bastet's brother, who was invoked to protect the household from all ill. It was believed that the stone tablet formed an impassable barrier to all venomous animals and evil spirits.

Bastet not only destroyed the sun-god's enemies but, as a moon-goddess and deity of the underworld, she also protected the dead from attack in the hereafter. As we know, she acquired this reputation largely through her ability to see in the dark. Magical ivory wands buried in tombs to give protection against supernatural evil sometimes had cat-headed terminals (Plate 4) or had cats engraved on them. The deities whose protection was invoked were often represented as subduing evil by eating venomous snakes. These wands are thought to have contained the horoscopes of the individuals with whom they were buried.

The cat has suffered as a result of its association with healing, for parts of its anatomy have frequently been used in folk-medicine. It was believed that if you killed a cat you were liable to be possessed by it, and that eating part of the animal was the only way to avert such a disaster.

The Japanese believed that a black cat could cure spasms if placed on the stomach of a sick person, and could also cure melancholia and even epilepsy.

Cat-fur has been used as a remedy for burns, and is still believed to be efficacious in the treatment of rheumatism. Many rheumatic people encourage a cat to settle on their shoulders, or to stretch out asleep on them at night.

The Dutch believed that inflammation can be cured by the application of the skin of a newly-killed cat. Elsewhere, cat-skin has been used to treat sore throats and hives.

The cat is specially noted as a healer of blindness, which is not surprising in view of its reputation as a seer. In parts of Scotland, people believe a cat has the power to bring vision to the mentally blinded, and their advice to "cast the cat over him" is given when someone appears to be deluded. Topsell gave the following prescription for physical blindness:

"Take the head of a black cat, which hath not a spot of another colour in it, and burn it to powder in an earthen pot, leaded or glazed within; then take this powder, and, through a quill, blow it thrice a day into thy eye; and if in the night any heat do thereby annoy thee, take two leaves of an oke, wet in cold water, and bind them to the eye, and so shall all pain flie away, and blindness depart, although it hath oppressed thee a whole year; and this medecine is approved by many physicians both elder and later."

The tail is, however, the part of the cat most widely used for healing. The cat's tail is a specially sensitive part of its anatomy and is responsible to some extent for its balance. (Manx cats keep their balance quite well without a tail, but apparently they are not much good at climbing.) The tail is an organ of the cat's self-expression and it has a complete language of its own. (The Greek word for cat, αἴλουρος, means" tail-waver".)

This is the part of the cat's body supposed to have the power to cure sties. It is generally accepted in English country districts that, if you rub a sty with a tom-cat's tail, the swelling will disappear. In Northamptonshire it is considered more effective to pluck a hair from the tip of a black cat's tail on the first night of a new moon, and draw it nine times across the swollen eyelid. In Cornwall, a spell is used in treatment of sties, for when you stroke the eye with the tail of a black cat you must say: "I poke thee, I don't poke thee, I toke the queff that's under the 'ee. Oh, qualy way; oh, qualy way."

The cat's tail is used in a rite designed to cure any kind of itch. A left-handed man must first find a black cat, and then whirl it three times around his own head. He should then prepare an ointment consisting of nine drops of blood taken from the cat's tail and the charred remains of nine roasted barley-corns. This unguent is applied with a gold wedding-ring as he walks thrice round the patient, invoking the Trinity. (We note again how closely the cat is associated with the esoteric threes and nines.) If the itch is known to be caused by shingles, all that is required is to smear over the affected area blood taken from a black cat's tail.

To cure whitlows, you must pass the tail of a black cat from the back of your hand down between the first and second fingers, then up again between the second and third, and down between the third and fourth fingers – on three successive nights. To remove warts, rub them with the tail of a tortoise-shell tom – but this treatment works only in the month of May.

Finally, we are told it is possible to avoid sickness in the

3. Solar cat slaying serpent of darkness *p. 8*

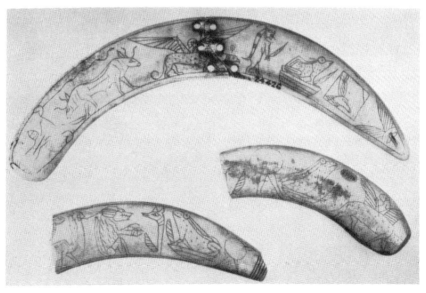

4. Magical ivory wand with cat-headed terminal *p. 28*

5. The Cat of Lapis Lazuli *p. 24*

6a. Talisman engraved with spell for exorcising poison from cats *p. 27*

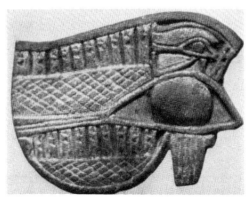

6b. Sacred eye amulet with nineteen cats inset *p. 23*

7. Hunting cat in a fowling scene *p. 32*

family altogether if you can bring yourself to cut off a black cat's tail and bury it under your doorstep.

The cat's healing-power appears, therefore, to have been focussed in its tail. The Celts apparently considered this part of its anatomy to be very precious and potent, for they believed that, if you were disrespectful enough to tread on a cat's tail, a serpent would come out and sting you.

The Hunter

The cat is a natural hunter. The Egyptian name "Bast" means "tearer" or "renderer", and the Indo-European root *ghad*, from which the Greek, Latin, Russian, Arabic, German and French words for "cat" derive, means "to grasp" or "to catch". And in the Jewish Talmud the cat is called "pouncer".

The cat does not, like a dog, chase its prey; it lies in wait for it and then pounces. Its patience is proverbial, for it will sit for hours silently watching its potential victim. In sacred works of Chinese Buddhism, the meditative attitude is likened to that of a cat which crouches, patiently and motionlessly vigilant, till the time comes for it to pounce on its prey, which are the "distractions".

In Egypt wild cats prowled about the marshlands in search of birds. Tomb-reliefs and paintings show marshland scenes with cats sitting in hiding among full-blown papyrus-heads, or creeping up the stems stalking birds.

Egyptians made use of the cat's hunting instinct, training it to catch and retrieve birds. Cats went with their masters on fowling expeditions and were let out of the boats into papyrus-thickets growing near the water's edge. Some tomb-paintings show yellow cats with black markings waiting impatiently in boats or among the reeds in the thickets alongside. Sometimes the hunter used a throwstick. He aimed it at the neck of the flying bird which, when it fell into the water or among the reeds, was retrieved by the highly-skilled hunting cat. Plate 7, which shows a typical fowling scene, was painted on an Egyptian tomb in about 1400 B.C. It depicts the owner of the tomb gliding through marshes accompanied by his lotus-gathering wife and daughter and their hunting cat which, perched on a papyrus stem, has succeeded in catching a bird.

The traditional victim of the cat's hunting instinct is, however, the mouse.

When Egyptians first tamed the cat, around 3000 B.C., it was in order to protect their grain from rodents. And cats still serve a useful purpose today by keeping our houses, stores, farms and ships free from vermin. Mice and rats are not, like snakes, poison-producing; but they are carriers of disease, who steal food and nibble and gnaw their way through our possessions. Worst of all they multiply at such a speed that the problem of uncontrollable hordes of rodents would soon be an overwhelming one if we had not the cat to solve it for us.

The cat has no difficulty in killing a mouse once it has caught it, and these grey timid creatures, who scuttle about as if they were always expecting to be pounced on, often appear almost to court disaster. Rats, on the other hand, can be fierce fighters, and cats often show great courage in tackling them. When a cat pounces on a large rat and all goes well, it deals skilfully with the problem, stunning the rat with a blow, and seizing it by the head in a vice-like grip. But the cat is often left panting with exhaustion after struggling with a rat, and is sometimes badly wounded by it.

Aesop believed that mousing was so much a part of cat-nature that, whatever other transformation might take place, this habit would always remain. One of his fables tells of a young man who fell in love with a cat, and felt so miserable and frustrated that he prayed to Venus to transform the cat into a beautiful woman. The goddess of love heard the young man's prayers and granted his request. He married the cat-girl, but their happiness was unfortunately short-lived for, when the bride lay in her husband's arms during their first night together, she suddenly saw a mouse appear from under the skirting-board, and instinctively sprang out of bed after it. Venus was furious that her sacred rites should be profaned by such indecent behaviour and, realizing that although this creature was outwardly a woman her nature was still that of a cat, she made her return to her old form.

Another of Aesop's cats leaves us in no doubt as to what it considered to be its rights, for it addressed a mouse:

> ". . . thou victim of my paw
> By well-established law."

A Russian legend brings out the advantages of this aspect of cat-nature: a dog and a cat were on guard at the gates of Paradise when Lucifer tried to creep back disguised as a mouse. The dog let him pass, but the cat pounced on him.

Cats and mice are often associated in legends concerned with the beginning of the world. According to one legend, not only did rodents precede cats but their existence was the reason for the cat's creation. At the time of the Flood, we are told, there were no cats. Noah (showing, one would have thought, extraordinary lack of foresight) took pairs of rats and mice into the Ark, with the result that it was soon overrun with vermin. Noah asked the lion, as king of the beasts, to do something about the situation. The lion sneezed, and from his nostrils emerged a pair of cats, which soon reduced the rodent population.

It has also been said that God created the cat, but that the mouse was Satan's creation; and the Devil's mouse did its best to destroy life once and for all by nibbling a hole in Noah's Ark. Fortunately it was caught by God's cat, and the hole was closed by a frog who crept into it.

A further account of the behaviour of God's cat and the Devil's mouse is given in an Italian legend about St Francis. When the recluse was living in his hermitage, he was plagued by Satan's efforts to distract him from prayer. Having failed many times the Devil sent, as a last resort, hundreds of mice to torment him. These diabolic animals overran the saint's cell, gnawing at his garments and nibbling at his feet. They were bringing St Francis's prayers to a close when suddenly out of his loose sleeve, sprang a cat. The speed and fury of the cat's onslaught was such that, out of the hundreds of mice, only two escaped, and this they did by hiding in a crack in the wall. The legend says that all descendants of this holy cat still sit motionless before holes and crevices, waiting to catch the fugitives.

Another legend accounts for the traditional enmity between cat and mouse. It describes how, at the beginning of the world, the sun and moon created all the animals. First the sun created a lion which was majestic and full of fire like himself. Then the moon, seeing that the gods were lost in admiration of the lion, was determined not to be outdone, so she produced a cat. Not only did the gods laugh at the obvious inferiority of the moon's creature, but the sun became very indignant that the moon should have dared to compete with him at all, and he created a mouse as a symbol of his contempt. Then the moon, angered by the mockery her efforts had provoked, created an eternal hatred between the cat and the mouse in a final effort to avenge herself on the sun.

Lunar mythology also closely associates the cat and the

mouse. We already know that Bastet was a goddess of the moon and as such she was, like Artemis (the Greek goddess with whom she was often identified), a huntress. Artemis has been called "The Madonna of the Silver Bow"; the silver bow was the crescent of the new moon and her shining arrows that split the darkness were moon-beams. The grey clouds of twilight were thought of as mice – those thieving, shadowy elements of the night which were dispersed by the darting paws of the radiant cat-moon.

The Hindu word for "cat" means "the cleanser". The cat is famous for its cleanliness, and the luminous cat-moon is the cleanser of the night, since she rids it of the shadowy grey mice-clouds.

(Mice have often been believed to be the souls of the departed – the ghosts who emerge from the underworld and wander in the twilight. Japanese fishermen, for instance, frequently take a tortoise-shell cat out to sea with them, for they believe that it not only keeps away rats – those notorious deserters of sinking ships – but also protects them from the "honourable ghosts" of their ancestors.)

Usually, in lunar mythology, the moon is thought of as a hunting cat, and a primitive American Indian tribe sees the waning moon as a victim of mice which, as animals of darkness, nibble at its sides until they have totally consumed it. But when the cat is identified with the sun, then the moon is sometimes likened to a white mouse. Some West African natives, for instance, explained a lunar eclipse by saying that a cat is eating the moon. They believed that the sun returns over the same route at night as it follows during the day, and that an eclipse means that the moon, having lost her way, has obstructed the sun and is being devoured by him. The natives tried to help the moon by ritual, using slow hand-clapping to persuade the solar cat to release her.

The Mother

Cats have a strong maternal instinct and never appear prouder and happier than with a litter of kittens. They lie contentedly suckling and purring with pleasure, and will protect their bright-eyed balls of fluff with great courage. A Hindu sect of southern India believes in what is known as the "cat-doctrine", which is contrasted with the "monkey-doctrine" found in northern India. These doctrines are based on the natural habits of the animals with their young. Adherents to the "cat-doctrine" believe in "salvation through grace", and are taught that God saves man as a cat takes up its kitten in its mouth without consideration of the free will of its young. (The teaching of believers in the "monkey-doctrine" is that man, in order to be saved, must embrace God as a baby monkey does its mother: the doctrine of "salvation by works".)

Egyptian amulets consisting of cat-families were very popular. Faience cats with blue and green glazes support an avalanche of kittens. The mother often sits hunched up with kittens perched on her head, tumbling down her back, squatting on her flexed forepaws, peeping out from between her legs, and there may be suckling kittens tucked away underneath her. Sometimes the mother extends a paw and rests it on the head of a kitten crouched in front of her. Bronze cat-families, on the other hand, tend to be more statuesque. The mother usually sits perfectly poised, with four kittens sitting in an orderly manner at her feet. Whereas the homely faience groups have a strong human appeal, the stylized bronze families inspire reverence for the quality of motherhood. Some bronzes are inscribed with an invocation to Bastet as a mother-goddess. Plate *11* shows, sculpted in stone, a sacred Egyptian cat lying peacefully among her kittens.

Cat-family amulets were specially popular in Egypt among young married couples. Newly-weds would decide how many children they wanted, and then find a cat-amulet with the appropriate number of kittens. The wife would either wear this symbol of motherhood suspended from a cord round her neck, or would hang it up on a wall in her house or in a nearby temple. She regularly prayed to the mother cat, as a representative of Bastet, the cat-goddess, asking to be sent the same number of babies as she had kittens.

Cats are very fertile animals, and queens are exceptionally highly sexed. When in season, the female rolls about on her back and yowls for hours until all the toms in the neighbour-hood have formed a circle around her. She will then satisfy each of them in turn.

Bastet became associated with all the mother-goddesses – those personifications of female productivity. She was identified with Isis as Mother Nature and the parent of all living creatures of the earth, sea and air; at Thebes, she was worshipped as the World Mother, Mut, whose temple was approached through a magnificent avenue of sphinxes. Some texts inscribed on the walls of the temple of Bubastis refer to Bastet as "mother" of some of the pharaohs. (When, for instance, the temple was first built, in the sixth dynasty, it was written of the reigning pharaoh that "his mother, Bastet, has nourished him".) Mut was queen of the gods and Egyptian queens wore her symbol, a vulture, on their crowns to repre-sent their royal motherhood. Where Bastet was worshipped as Mut, her cat-head was replaced by that of a vulture.

Although Bastet was worshipped as the feminine principle of nature, later periods of Egyptian history celebrated her as a goddess of fertility and generative power. The cat-goddess was the female counterpart of Ptah, the sun-god and ancient "giver of life" whose rays produced fecundity in nature.

Bast and Isis, like the Greek Demeter and the Celtic Cerridwen, were earth-goddesses who gave birth to the spirit of corn, and all four deities took the form of a cat. (In New Guinea, where yams were a staple food, the ritual game of "cat's-cradle" was played to promote the growth of crops. Everyone joined in, the children imitating the adults, and when the "cat's-cradles" had been completed the strings were used for tying up the yam-stalks. Sometimes pieces of these "cat's-cradle" strings were only hung on the first few sticks, or people just scattered them carelessly over their gardens. But the purpose of the rite was always the same, for it was intended to ensure – by sympathetic magic – that the yam-leaves spread, and that their stalks intertwined to best advantage.)

As a goddess of the fields, Bastet was also identified with the Nordic Freya, a sun-goddess of fruitfulness and love. Freya, who travelled through the country in a chariot drawn by a pair of cats, caused the seeds to swell and to sprout. She would bless and give special protection to the harvests of those farmers who put out milk in their cornfields for her divine cats.

Freya blessed all lovers, and Friday (Freya's Day) was the most auspicious day for weddings. Cats are still believed to foretell whether or not a marriage will take place, and their appearance on wedding-days is still considered to be auspicious.

Egyptian cat-family amulets were not only believed to promote fertility, but also to give protection to pregnant women and to those children already born to them. Bastet exercised a special influence over the birth-chamber. It is not known exactly what such goddesses did: some acted as midwives and others as nurses, but many seem only to have presided. Bastet was often depicted near a couch in a lying-in chamber, and her presence was obviously considered important to both mother and child.

In her identification with Hathor, the cow-goddess, Bastet established herself as a great Nourisher, for it was the white moon-cat, like the white moon-cow, who gave and sustained vegetable life, nourishing the crops with her fructifying rain.

During the periods of drought primitive people resorted to magic as a means of producing the rain so essential to their lives. Cats have been widely used as rain-makers. In southern Celebes rain was ritually produced by tying a cat into a sedan-chair and carrying it three times round a parched field. It would be drenched with water trained on it from bamboo squirts, and when it mewed the natives chanted, "O Lord, let rain fall on us."

Cats were also used in a Malayan rain-making ritual. A woman first placed an inverted earthenware pan on her head, then set it on the ground, filled it with water and bathed a cat in it till it nearly drowned. Similarly, in Java, cats were bathed or ducked in pools in order to produce rain, and those taking part were carried in procession to music.

A black cat was used as a rain-maker in Sumatra, and the colour of the cat was significant in this case, for it was believed that, by sympathetic magic, the blackness would darken the sky with rain-clouds. Here, village women waded into the river, taking with them a black cat which they threw in and forced to swim. Eventually the bedraggled animal was allowed to escape to the bank, but it was pursued all the way by splashing women. At a place called Kota Gadang, there was a stone believed to have the power to draw water down from the sky, simply because it resembled a cat. During periods of drought this cat-stone was smeared with the blood of fowls, then rubbed and perfumed with incense while a charm was uttered over it.

In many parts of the British Isles, cats are still believed to foretell rain as, for instance, when they sneeze or wash themselves behind their ears with a wet forepaw.

The Egyptian cow-goddess not only nourished the living but also the souls of the dead. In the underworld, Hathor leaned out of the trunk of a sycamore tree, and offered food and drink to passing ghosts. Isis, with whom Bastet was also identified, was the loving, protecting mother of the dead; and we have already seen how the cat was associated with funerary rites, assisting the deceased in their return to the womb of the earth-mother.

The Seed

The tom-cat is an animal of considerable sexual activity. The phallic aspect of the cat is emphasized in its identification with the fiery asp of the sun (Plate *10* shows an Egyptian cat-headed priest with a snake), and it was believed that the penetrating rays of the solar cat produced fecundity in nature. The solar cat is both father and son, for it enters into the earth and fertilizes it, then emerges from the ground as the spirit of corn.

When Osiris was identified with Ra, the solar cat, he was worshipped as the deity of vegetation. A bronze group in the Cairo Museum shows Osiris enthroned between Nefertem (Bastet's son) and Horus the child, with a female cat lying at his feet and a worshipper kneeling in front of them.[1] An

---

[1] It has, however, been suggested that it was Sekhmet who originally occupied this throne.

amulet in the Langton Collection depicts a lion-headed goddess wearing a disk and sacred asp, flanked each side by a standing Osiris and carrying a seated cat on each shoulder. Another shows Osiris standing holding the royal crook and cat-o'-nine-tails, with a cat seated in front of his right foot. Osiris personified the corn spirit and was commonly known as "The Seed". In the temple of Isis at Philae, the dead body of Osiris is represented with stalks of corn springing from it, which are being watered by a priest with a pitcher. The myth of Osiris tells how the god was murdered by Set, the devil, and pieces of his body were scattered throughout Egypt. In an annual harvest-ritual commemorating the death, dis-memberment and resuscitation of Osiris, he was often repre-sented by a cat – an animal with which he was closely associated through his daughter, Bastet, and which seems to have been suited in many ways to incarnate the spirit of corn.

In European vegetation-rites Osiris, the corn-spirit, and the cat were one. Sometimes an imaginary cat was used (the close of the harvest being known as "killing the cat"), but more often a live cat was placed in the last bundle of corn, where it was thrashed and struck dead by the flails. The body of the animal would be cooked and eaten sacramentally by the harvesters as the body of the murdered god.

In the Vosges mountains the crop was known as "the cat", and was described as "fat" or "lean" according to whether the corn was abundant or poor. The man who cut the last handful of grain was regarded as the "catcher of the corn-cat", and was presented with a bouquet or a small fir-tree decorated with ribbons. In Scotland, a handful of reaped grain or straw, which has been laid on the ground without being bound into a sheaf, is known as a "cat".

In Dauphiné, when reaping began, a cat was decorated with ribbons, flowers and ears of corn, and was named "the cat of the ball-skin". If a reaper was injured, the cat was persuaded to lick his wounds. When the reaping was over the workers danced and made merry round the corn-cat, until eventually the girls would ritually strip it of all its decorations. In Silesia, the reaper who cut the last corn was called the "tom-cat", while a second reaper was called the "she-cat", and both were enveloped in ryestalks and provided with long plaited tails. It was then their privilege to chase and beat everyone in sight.

In Amiens a cat was sacrificed to ensure the welfare of the crops the following year. When the harvest was about to be completed, the word went round the fields, "They are going to kill the cat," and the reapers repaired to the farmyard and watched a cat put to death. In Bohemia a cat was sometimes killed and buried in a cornfield to prevent evil spirits damaging the next year's crop.

According to the Chinese *Book of Rites* (the *Lî Kî*), Chinese farmers worshipped a cat-god called *Li Shou*. After the crop had been gathered in, peasants indulged in an orgiastic harvest-festival and made sacrifices to the cats "who had devoured rats and mice which would otherwise have injured the crops". (Osiris was also a protector of the corn as well as a personification of it.)

The phallic aspect of the cat was powerfully emphasized in a polytheistic Egyptian bronze which appeared in a sale at Sotherby's some years ago. This figure had a winged body which stood on a crocodile, and its emblems included those of Osiris and Bastet. Distinguishing it from all other such figures was a cat's head in the place of sexual organs.

During one of the earliest stages of cultural development, when people worshipped earth- and lunar-deities, the moon was thought of as masculine. Women believed that if they exposed themselves to moon-beams they were liable to become pregnant, and Khensu, Bastet's moon-son, was said to make women fruitful and to cause the human seed to grow in the womb.

The supreme deity of the Mochica people, who lived along the northern coast of Peru, was a god called *Ai apaec*, a feline being developed from an ancient cat-god. *Ai apaec* was usually portrayed as a wrinkled-faced old man with long fangs and cat's whiskers, and Mochica pottery vessels show his human and feline faces back to back. *Ai apaec* was a farmer, hunter, fisherman and physician, and in particular he presided over human copulation, ensuring that it bore fruit.

An Egyptian papyrus states that when the moon is up "couplings and conceptions abound". Certainly cats appear to be most passionate at the full moon. Osiris and Bastet, as we have seen, were both lunar deities, and the cat, as their representative, was held responsible for human fecundity as well as for the fruitfulness of the earth.

Perhaps the cat's association with human conception is responsible for the belief that black cats turning up at weddings are omens of good luck. There is a Scottish superstition that, if a tom-cat ejects semen while jumping over food, any woman who unknowingly eats it will conceive kittens (hence perhaps the expression, "I nearly had kittens!"). In 1654, a Scottish court tried the case of a woman who confessed that she had "cats in her bellie", and had made unsuccessful attempts to procure abortion. It appeared that, in those days, pregnant women in pain were often worried by witches who assured them that their misery was due to having kittens in their wombs, and that this condition could be remedied by use of magical potions.

The Virgin

The cat is the cleanest of all animals. It spends hours grooming itself and its kittens with its tongue, and any suggestion of contamination by human beings is followed by urgent and strenuous licking.

The only way in which the cat can possibly be thought of as virgin is if the word is used in its broadest sense, for although it is usually taken as referring to a person innocent of sexual intercourse, more deeply it means someone who is "unpossessed" and has remained "unsullied" by sex. The Immaculate Womb of the Virgin Mary has been thought of as an abyss in which nothing leaves a stain: although it gives birth to all things, as the queen of heaven gives birth to the sun, moon and stars, it remains eternally virgin and spotless. The fertility-goddesses were always considered to be virgin, for the Great Mother was a personification of the womb of nature. To this goddess the male was an anonymous fertilizing agent, and the temple prostitutes, who were priestesses of the Great Mother, although prepared to give themselves to any man, belonged to no man.

In spite of the fact that Bastet was a goddess of fecundity, love, maternity and of the birth-chamber, she was also, like the Greek cat-goddess, Artemis, worshipped as a virgin. The cat-moon was the purifier of the night, cleansing it of dark shadows and thieving mice. The emblem of Mut, the mother-goddess with whom Bastet was often identified, was, as we know, a vulture. But the vulture was a symbol of *virgin* mother-hood, for it was popularly believed to be parthenogenetic.

When the tide of Christianity swept all before it, the Madonna took possession of the sanctuaries of the old fertility-goddesses. Bastet, Isis, Demeter, Cerridwen (all of whom had taken cat-form) were the virgin mothers of the spirit of corn, and the Virgin Mary who superseded them appeared as the Divine Mother of the "Bread of Life".

Plate *12* shows Baroccio's painting, the "Madonna of the Cat". The cat is ginger and white, and it is being tantalized by the young John the Baptist who has a bird in his hand. Several artists have included a cat in their Holy Families, probably as a reference to the Christian legend according to which a cat gave birth in the Bethlehem stable at the same moment as did the Virgin Mary. Leonardo da Vinci produced numerous sketches of the Virgin and Child with a kitten, and a cat appears in many paintings of the birth of the Virgin and of the Annunciation.

Cats as we know them are essentially home-loving animals, and throughout the winter they are apt to take possession of the hearth. In Rome the guardian of the hearth and home was Vesta, a virgin goddess whose priestesses, the famous vestal virgins, tended the sacred fire in a Roman sanctuary. A virgin always to be found on the hearth in folk-tales is Cinderella (or whichever variant of her name is used), and she is closely associated with the cat. The tale exists in many different languages and, although it varies considerably in detail, is basically always about a good-natured girl whose beauty is hidden and who is ill-treated by her family. Eventually her beauty is revealed, her goodness rewarded, and she makes a marriage which is the envy of all. The oldest version of the tale is Italian, and in this the despised stepdaughter who lives on the kitchen-hearth is known as "Cinders-Cat".

In the English fairy-tale called "Catskin", the unwanted maiden warmed herself at the kitchen-fire, covered from head to foot in a catskin. Although she spent her days sweeping cinders from the hearth and cleaning pigsties, when the king gave a ball she managed to slip out and appeared among the nobility as a shining beauty. A handsome young nobleman fell in love with her and, realizing that, although "cat without, she was queen within", he married her.

In a Danish version, a cat asks the ill-treated heroine for a saucer of milk and, in spite of having been thrashed twice before for doing so, she feeds the animal for the third time. The cat then swells and pushes off its skin, which the maiden uses as a cloak. Later, the cat provides her with beautiful dresses, and finally is itself transformed into a handsome prince who is a brother of the king and soon marries the heroine. (There is an Irish version of the story in which the fairy godmother is a cat; and, in an old tale from Brittany, the cat provides the ragged girl with beautiful dresses and is eventually transformed into a prince.)

The most popular version of the story, and the one with which we are all familiar, bears the English title "Cinderella", and is based on Perrault's "Cendrillon". In this version there is no mention of a cat – only of a virgin on a hearth, and of mice and rats. (It is interesting to note that in Sicily the cat, which keeps the house free of vermin, is sacred to St Martha, the patroness of domestic virtue.) Another account of this story is called "The Hearth Cat".

When the virgin cat-goddess is darkened by smoke and ashes she reminds one of those black Madonnas that are to be seen in French and Italian churches.

Some people have believed that, after death, the souls of "old maids" take possession of black cats. In the thirteenth century cats were the only animals allowed in English nunneries, for the *Ancren Riwle* of 1205 instructed: "Ye, my dear sisters, shall have no beast but a cat."

The virgin is, at least symbolically, an independent woman. Cats are famed for their independence, which distinguishes them from all other "tamed" animals. Although they have

8. Bastet, the cat-goddess *p. 15*

9a. Japanese temple cat-instrument *p. 55*

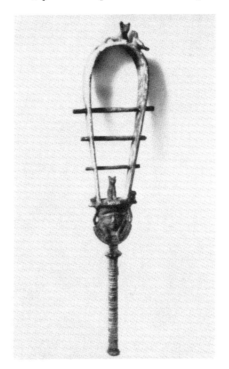

9b. Sistrum decorated with sacred cats *p. 56*

10. Egyptian cat-headed priest with a snake *p. 40*

11. Sacred mother-cat suckling kittens *p. 36*

12. "Madonna of the Cat" *p. 45*

associated with human beings for centuries, they are still as self-possessed as they were in the jungle. Unlike much larger and stronger animals, they have never become servile, but remain indifferent both to man's will and his favours. They accept the comforts but reject the bondage of domesticity. They hunt and wander alone, not in packs, for they are not, like men, gregarious. Their solitariness and detachment have been immortalized by Rudyard Kipling in "The Cat that Walked by Itself"; and in Chinese Buddhism the cat appears as a symbol of self-possession.

At various times the independence of the cat has led to its official use as a symbol of human liberty. The Roman goddess of liberty has a cat lying at her feet. Roman legions setting out to defend their freedom had cats blazoned on their banners: one marched with a green cat on a silver ground, another carried a red cat on a pink shield, and an alpine troop bore a cat with one eye and one ear.

In Switzerland, too, the cat was a symbol of liberty; and the Dutch, who had struggled so long to gain independence, chose the cat as their ensign. The first French Republic placed the cat at the side of the statue of liberty, and added it to its shield of arms. Prud'hon, the Republican artist, painted an allegorical picture of the French Constitution which now hangs in Dijon. In this painting, Liberty holds a broken chain and a pike surmounted by a Phrygian cap, while at her feet sits a large, handsome cat. Many artists copied Prud'hon in depicting Liberty with a broken chain and a cat, but the reign of the cat, as a symbol of French liberty, ended with that of the Republic.

The cat, through its independence, also became associated with the law, as an instrument designed to liberate the oppressed. St Yves, the patron saint of lawyers who was represented giving alms to the poor, was sometimes shown with a cat. As we know the ears of the Egyptian figures of Bastet were often decorated with the "feather of Maat" (see Frontispiece) who was the goddess of law and justice. And, in a magical text in the *Book of the Dead*, we find the following address to the cat-goddess: "O Bastet, who come forth from the sanctuary, I have not winked at *injustice*."

The Talisman

Cats protected Egyptian houses and farms from rodents, and above all from poisonous snakes. We have already seen what great faith the Egyptians had in the cat's capacity to protect them, in both this world and the next, from natural and supernatural evil.

The Chinese believed that cats had the power to detect evil spirits and put them to flight. It was because of this reputed faculty (based on the cat's ability to see in the dark) that a cat-spirit was worshipped in some parts of China. In sixth-century Japan sacrifices were made to the "Guardian of the Manuscripts", a sacred cat whose responsibility it was to guard papyrus-rolls stored in temples against mice and rats, and Russian peasants used to put a cat into a new baby's cradle to drive away evil spirits from the infant.

In Europe tri-coloured cats were thought to have the power to protect households against destruction by fire. And many cats have been walled up in new buildings, allegedly as safeguards against catastrophe.

The talisman is a magical image which has the power to avert or repel evil. And where the cat was believed to give powerful protection and to ward off unpleasantness of every kind, its image became widely used as a talisman when no living cat was available. Cats carved over Theban temples, for example, gave them protection. The Japanese used cat-images to guard mortuary chambers against rats, and Plate *15* shows the famous seventeenth-century wood-carving of a cat, sleeping among peonies over the door of a shrine in the temple of Nikko. This cat was credited with having driven all vermin from the temple.

Cats were widely used by the Chinese for protecting silk-worms. When the season came for feeding the worms, silk-worm farmers bought up all the cats they could find, believing that their presence was in itself sufficient to keep off the rats. In the absence of live cats, however, they stuck pictures of "silkworm-cats" on their walls, in the belief that the image had the same power as a live cat to protect the worms.

The Chinese also used clay pictures of sitting cats with staring eyes to keep evil influences at bay. They were placed on top of walls or beneath the eaves of houses, and the picture of a magic cat is still to be seen repelling demons from the roof of a rest-house in Shanghai.

The cat-amulet was more widely used in Egypt than in any other part of the world. People in all classes of society wore little pierced or ringed images of Bastet's cats suspended round their necks to safeguard them wherever they went; we have already seen that innumerable cat-effigies, carved in bronze, faience, wood and precious stones, were buried in walls and under floors with the intention of protecting the house or temple.

Some amulets seem to have depended on the image alone to give protection, for the cat-image was itself dynamic, whether standing or sitting as a goddess laden with her emblems, or enshrined, or combined with the god of fertility, or just being a mother surrounded by her young. To other cat-amulets, however, the power of the word was added.

In Egypt the power of the word was considered to be very

great. It was believed, for instance, that a substantial bond existed between a man and his name, so that it was virtually a part of him. Primitive peoples have always been reluctant to disclose their names, for if their enemies knew them they could, by the use of magic, injure people through their names. The name was also regarded as expressing the nature of a thing, and the name of a deity was believed to be his manifestation and was treated with great veneration. Since kings and deities were focuses of power, their names inscribed on amulets added the power of royalty or divinity to that inherent in the image. Furthermore, power was contained not only in single words but also in rhythmic groups of words – hence magical formulae, spells and incantations. (Spells often took the form of invocation of deities who were chosen because of incidents in their own lives, as in the case of the spell to cure a scorpion-sting, in which Bastet was invoked and reference made to her personal experience of a similar nature.)

Cat-amulets, the power of which has been strengthened by inscriptions, include lion-headed goddesses inscribed with the name of Bastet, scarabs engraved with a cat combined with the name of Bastet, and cat-families bearing an invocation to Bastet as a mother-deity, which were used for protection of children. Finally, there is a talisman consisting of a seated cat wearing a collar of beads and inscribed with the magical formula: "May Bastet, Lady of Ankh-taui, give protection." In all of these, the power of the image of the cat has been increased by the addition of the cat-divinity's power.

The Egyptian talisman was also used to protect the dead. There were the sacred eye amulets (utchats) which put the deceased under the protection of the sun and moon, both of which were personified by the cat deity. Utchats full of cats, and small faience or bronze cat-figures, guarded the deceased; while cat-headed ivory wands evoked the protection of the gods engraved on them. Many amulets found on mummies were inscribed with words of power, and with spells which would prove useful to the deceased in the hereafter.

The Charm

"Charm", "talisman" and "amulet" are words which tend to be used rather loosely and interchangeably, and the difference between them is largely one of emphasis. It is claimed that all three have the power both to repel evil and attract good; but whereas the repelling powers of the amulet and talisman are stressed, in the case of the charm more emphasis is laid on its power to attract good fortune. The word "charm" originally meant "incantation", but later it was stretched to include any object or action which was believed to possess the power of the incantation or spell.

Live cats have been used as charms, and in Chinese shops are kept collared and chained. The older and uglier these cats are, the greater the luck they bring their owners and it is assumed that, if they escaped, prosperity would go with them.

In Europe, black cats predominate as lucky charms. In Scotland and Ireland, a stray tortoise-shell cat settling in one's home is a good omen, and in some places a cat with double claws is said to bring good luck. There is, furthermore, a Buddhist belief that light-coloured cats ensure that there will always be silver in the house, and dark-coloured cats that there will always be gold.

As cats became increasingly prized as luck-bringers, the problem arose as to how they could be acquired. An eighteenth-century magazine gave the following account of a charm by means of which numerous cats could be captured:

"In the new moon gather the herb Nepe and dry it in the

heat of the sun; gather vervain in the hour 8, and only expose it to the air while the moon is under the earth. Hang these together in a net in a convenient place, and when one of them has scented it her cry will soon call those about within hearing; and they will rant and run about leaping and capering to get at the net, which must be hung or placed so that they cannot accomplish it, or they will tear it in pieces."

(Vervain is sometimes called the "holy herb" from its use in ancient sacred rites. It was supposed to cure the bites of rabid animals, and to arrest diffusion of the poison.) Near Bristol there is a "Field of Cats", so called because a large number of cats were drawn together here by this charm.

A further problem arose for those who, having acquired good luck in the form of a cat, then found that they had to move house. The charm most commonly used to make a cat settle in a new home was the buttering of its paws.

In Japan, a popular charm is a "beckoning" cat, and the following legend is attached to a cat-shrine in the grounds of the temple known as *Gotoku-ji*. This temple was originally a very poor one, no more than a thatched hut run by poverty-stricken and half-starved monks. The master-priest had a cat of which he was fond, and shared with it such little food as he had. One day the cat squatted by the roadside and, when half-a-dozen *Samurai* appeared on splendid horses, it looked up at them and raised one of its paws to its ear, as if it were beckoning to them. The noble cavaliers pulled up and, as the cat continued to beckon, they followed it into the temple. Torrential rain forced them to stay for a while, so the priest gave them tea and expounded Buddhist doctrine. After this one of the *Samurai* – Lord Li – regularly visited the old priest to receive religious instruction from him. Eventually, Li endowed the temple with a large estate and it became the property of his family. Visitors who pass under the temple's impressive gateways, walk through its broad avenues of towering trees and enjoy the beautifully laid-out gardens, discover, near the cemetery of the Li Family, the little shrine of the beckoning cat – which, it is said, still draws pilgrims from all parts of Tokyo.

As in the case of talismanic cats, the live animal used as a charm was often replaced by its image, which was found equally effective. At the entrances to their shops and restaurants, the Japanese place clay, papier-mâché or wooden figures of a seated cat with one paw raised to the side of its face. Such cats are believed to promote prosperity, their beckoning paws inviting passers-by to come in and do business.

Sometimes this charm consists of a single porcelain beckoning cat; sometimes an earthenware one will have kittens crawling over her. Plate 16 shows a seventeenth-century beckoning mother-cat, carved in pearwood and signed on its base with the artist's name. The beckoning kittens would presumably add to the power of the charm.

The beckoning cat provides a good example of the way in which the use of charms and talismans overlaps, for although it is most commonly used to attract good fortune it can also be trusted to ward off evil. This charm is used, for instance (like the "silkworm-cat"), by cocoon-breeders to protect the silkworms against rats. It is widely used as a children's toy, and they wear beckoning cats tied round their waists to protect them against pain and sickness. The Japanese appear to share with Egyptians belief in the power of the word, for not only the image of the beckoning cat, but also the ideograph representing its name, is regarded as efficacious.

Egyptian cat-charms are of course prolific, and many have already been described under the classification of amulets. There were the fertility charms in the form of cat-families, which often bore invocations to Bastet as a mother. The "sacred eyes" were not only apotropaic, for they were the eyes of Horus the sun-god who was the source of health and happiness.

Bastet had much more than good luck to bestow. Probably because of her identification with the sun-eye, she was thought of as the "Possessor of Life". A tomb-inscription proclaims that she "gives life, prosperity and health every day, and long life and beautiful old age". A scarab is inscribed, "Bastet, maker of all gifts"; and a lion-headed, human-bodied figure in the Langton Collection is inscribed, "Bastet, who gives life and prosperity." Sometimes the power of the charm is directed towards an individual, as in the case of a seated cat which is wearing an engraved utchat as a pendant, and has its base inscribed with the words: "May Bastet, the great Lady of Bubastis, cause Haremhab . . . to live"; and also of a crouching cat in white limestone, inscribed, "May Bastet give a happy New Year to Pedubaste."

No wonder cats are thought of as charms, since the goddess they represent has so much good fortune to bestow!

The Musician

One mixed blessing bestowed on human beings by cats is their music. It is said that their mewing contains sixty-three notes, and the name "cats' melody" that we give to discordant sounds has arisen from the yowling and caterwauling that split the silence of moonlit nights.

The cat has always been connected with music and, perhaps because its body vibrates with deep purring, with musical instruments. It is, of course, by nature a player – as dragonflies, mice and birds know to their cost. A legend explains that the first cat was an offspring of the union of a lion and a monkey, and that it was from the monkey it inherited its playfulness. No one seems to know why the cat is specially associated with fiddles. It may be something to do with the fact that the strings of violins are made of so-called "catgut", a tough cord which is made from the intestines of animals, but is usually taken from sheep and never from cats. No satisfactory explanation has been given as to why violin-strings should ever have acquired this name. The word may possibly be a corruption of "kit-gut", "kit" being an old word for a small fiddle.

Cat-orchestras have been a popular subject among illustrators of children's books, who frequently depict cats conducting, singing and playing every kind of instrument. At one time there were people who dressed up cats and exhibited them as "musicians". The last public cat-concert appears to have been given by a Venetian in London in 1789.

In the fifteenth century, the terrible cat-organs were invented. Twenty cats would be confined in narrow cases in which they were unable to move. Their tails, which protruded, were tied by cords attached to the keyboard of the organ, so that when the keys were pressed the cords were raised and the cats' tails pulled to make them mew. Later this organ was improved on, and various other instruments were constructed whose music was provided by tortured cats. It is difficult to understand how the cries of suffering animals could have been found entertaining by people for several centuries.

In the absence of real cats, their images have been used to produce music. A collection of musical instruments in New York includes an ancient Japanese temple-instrument, consisting of what has been called a tiger but looks like a cat, lying on a decorated box carved from a solid block of wood (Plate 9a). A raised saw-toothed spine runs down the centre of the cat's back, and a character is cut on its forehead which means "pleasure". At certain points in temple-services a rattling sound was produced by scraping the cat's spine with a stick, and its head was struck on the "pleasure" mark.

Music is also produced from the body of a cat in a Javanese instrument called a *saron*, which is made in the form of a cat sitting with outstretched paws and open mouth. Parallel bars on its back are struck with a rod, as a xylophone is played. Presumably the open mouth of the cat is intended to give the impression that the music is vocal.

The sistrum – a kind of rattle consisting of a loop pierced by four loose rods and mounted on a handle – is an instrument closely associated with cats. Not only was the sistrum an emblem unique to the cat-goddess, but a sacred cat usually formed part of it, either perching on top of the handle or crowning the loop. Single cats, mostly, adorn sistra, but some suckle a kitten or play with a bird. Often the sistrum handle carries the head of Hathor, the cow-goddess (Plate *9b*).

Sistra were widely used in Egyptian religious rites and when, shortly before the Christian era began, the worship of Isis was introduced into Italy, these instruments were used in Roman ritual, too. At Portici (near Vesuvius), two paintings were found showing a priest of Isis and a kneeling woman rattling sistra. The central object of the rite appears to be a cat seated on an outsize sistrum.

The cats found on sistra were presumed to be incarnations of Bastet (the Roman one exemplifying the common identification of Isis with her daughter). An amulet showing a cat with a lute is inscribed, "Bast-Re is the Lord of Happiness". But it was through her merging with the cow-goddess, Hathor, who was known as "The Lady of Music and Mistress of Song", that Bastet was worshipped as a goddess of pleasure. Hathor was described as "merry as Bastet", and, in the orgiastic festival which they shared, there was much singing, dancing, shouting, rattling of sistra, clashing of crotola and beating of drums.

No one who has observed the luxuriating sensuality of a cat can doubt that it is a pleasure-loving animal. The grace and co-ordination of its movements are only equalled, in the human sphere, by dancers. But the only time a cat can strictly be said to dance is on those occasions when it prances around and leaps in the air, apparently partnered by a ghost though in fact by an unseen insect.

A bas-relief in a Roman museum shows a woman playing a lyre and trying to teach a cat to dance. She has hung two dead birds from a branch just above the cat's head, so that it prances about on its hind legs.

Dancing women participating in the Sebasian Mysteries often carried cat-crowned sistra. (They were used in Circle Dances, which symbolized the motion of the planets round the sun and formed part of the sacred rites of star-worshippers.) Dancers and singers were present at most Egyptian feasts. Funeral processions accompanying the statue of the deceased were headed by dancers who moved to the music of singers bringing up the rear. An Egyptian temple-carving shows singers and dancers facing each other across a table at a funeral feast. Behind the singers stands a little pillar with the head of a cat representing Bastet as the presiding deity; and near by is a figure of a nude dwarf, which would probably represent the god, Bes, a divinity of music, dance and pleasure.

Amulets often combine Bes's image with that of Bastet and sacred cats. One shows Bastet, with a cat's head, legs and tail, carrying her three usual emblems. On her right stands the figure of Bes playing a lyre, while to her left crouches a cat which is biting the head of a bird. Another amulet shows Bes playing a lute, with cats seated as supporters on both sides of him.

It is significant that all three cat-associated deities of music and pleasure were also connected with war. Bastet wore the aegis of Sekhmet, the goddess of battle who belched fire; Hathor was the most bloodthirsty of war-goddesses, and Bes was a terrifying god of slaughter. It will be recalled that cat-sistra were used militarily in Egypt as a means of summoning the troops. It seems extraordinary that an instrument symbolizing harmony should be used to summon the forces of war and discord, but perhaps this fact is related to that dissonance for which the "cats' melody" is justly famed.

The Servant

We have seen how cats have served men in protecting their houses and crops from destruction by rodents, and their persons from death by poisonous snakes, and how the cat has been believed not only to ward off evil, but to help the oppressed, and bring health and prosperity into human lives. In fairy-tales cats bring money, jewels and treasures of all kinds, including valuable qualities such as feline shrewdness and resourcefulness – all of which are put to the service of mankind.

In the Middle Ages cats were believed to have the power to produce money. According to a witch-remedy, if you buried a black cat with a gold piece and closed its eyes with two black beans, you would find that you always had money.

An Italian fairy-story tells of a woman who had many children but hardly any money at all. One day a fairy appeared to her and told her that, if she climbed to the top of a certain mountain, she would find an enchanted palace which was inhabited by cats who gave alms. So the woman made her way up to the palace and was met at the door by a kitten who let her in. She immediately set about providing help that was needed: sweeping out their rooms, lighting fires, washing dishes, drawing water, making beds and baking cakes for the cats of the enchanted palace. Eventually she was brought before the crowned King of the Cats and asked him for alms. The king pulled a golden chain which rang a golden bell, and asked the cats how the woman had treated them. On hearing of the generous help she had given, he ordered the cats to fill her apron with gold coins. (This story of alms-giving cats recalls the picture of the lawyers' patron saint, Yves, who is depicted, with a cat at his side, giving alms to the poor.)

The well-known English story of Dick Whittington is of a cat who brought wealth and jewels to an oppressed boy. Through her, he won a wife, fame as the Lord Mayor of London and, eventually, a knighthood.

There is a Celtic myth, which tells of a cat with many treasures, whose moral shows what happens if these treasures are stolen, instead of received as a gift. A young man called Maeldune, the adopted son of an Irish queen, set out in a boat one day with his three foster-brothers to avenge the death of his father. They came to an island on which stood a lofty stronghold with white walls surrounded by white houses, all of which were open and deserted. The young men entered the best of the houses but found nothing in it except a small cat leaping about among four stone pillars.

Ignored by the cat, the youths discovered that round the wall of the house there were three rows of dazzling treasures. The first row consisted of silver and gold brooches; the second of silver and gold necklaces, and the third of swords with silver and gold hilts. In the middle of the house they found an ox roasting on a fire, and large vessels full of fermented wine. Maeldune asked the cat if the food was all for them, and, when it looked at him for a minute then returned to its game, they were reassured, and ate and drank and slept.

Unfortunately, just before they left, and in spite of

Maeldune's warning, the third brother could not resist taking one of the necklaces. They had only got as far as the stronghold, when the cat leapt through the thief "like a fiery arrow" and the young man was burned to a heap of ashes.

Maeldune put the necklace back in its place, spoke soothingly to the cat and, flinging the ashes of his foster-brother into the sea, returned to the boat and made for home.

In the well-known French tale of "Puss in Boots", the cat's cunning and resourcefulness are emphasized. His loyal service and ingenuity turn a poor miller's son into the wealthy husband of a king's daughter.

Perhaps one of the richest of all fairy-tales is the French story of "The White Cat", in which a female cat helps a youngest son to perform tasks which eventually bring him kingship.

This story tells of an ageing king who set tasks for his three sons in order to establish which should become his heir. The first demand he made was for an intelligent little dog, and he promised that the son who acquired the handsomest animal should succeed him.

The youngest son, a handsome, courageous and accomplished prince, set off on his own, and each day he bought a number of dogs, keeping only the most attractive. One night, however, he lost his way in a dark forest, and a sudden thunderstorm soaked him to the skin. After walking blindly for some time, he saw a glimmer of light through the trees, which gave him hope of finding shelter until the morning.

Pushing through the trees towards the light, he came to a magnificent castle with golden gates studded with carbuncles, and walls made of translucent porcelain. When he rang the bell, the gate was opened by bodiless hands which, as he hesitated to enter, gently pushed him forward. He was led through sixty rooms, whose walls of lapis lazuli, mother-ofpearl and many other jewels were illuminated by thousands of lights. Eventually he came to a large easy chair by a fire and sat down. Bodiless hands then stripped the prince of his wet clothes, and dressed him in rich robes embroidered with jewels. After the hands had powdered, curled, perfumed and so adorned him that he looked more handsome than Adonis, they led him into a magnificent hall whose walls were hung with paintings of all the most famous cats of history.

The prince sat at a table which was laid for two, and watched several cats take their place in a small orchestra. One held a music-book, another beat time with a roll of paper, and the rest had little guitars. They began to mew in different tones, and they sat down to dinner.

Then the prince saw a tiny figure, completely covered with a black veil, enter the hall. She was preceded by two cats in mourning, wearing cloaks and swords, and a long train of cats carrying rat-traps full of rats and cages full of mice. When the little figure draped in black approached him and lifted its veil, he saw the most beautiful white cat that ever existed. She appeared youthful but very melancholy, and on her paw she wore a bracelet, set with a miniature of a young man exactly like the prince. The White Cat, who had the power of speech, welcomed the prince to her palace and the entire company sat down to dinner.

After dinner, which was followed by a ballet performed by cats and monkeys, the prince was led by the hands to a bed-room hung with brilliantly coloured butterfly-wings and the feathers of rare birds. He had not been asleep for long, how-ever, when he was awakened, lifted out of bed and dressed in a hunting-habit. The White Cat was going to hunt and wished the prince to accompany her. In the courtyard below, he saw at least five hundred cats making preparations for the hunt (Plate 13). He was placed on a wooden horse whose saddle was decorated with gold and diamonds, while the White Cat rode on a monkey. The hunting cats easily outran the rabbits and hares; kittens climbed trees after birds, and the monkey carried the White Cat to heights where an eagle nested.

The prince spent all his days enjoying the company of the White Cat. Sometimes he fished, hunted or watched a ballet with her. They always dined together, and the beautiful cat composed sonnets full of passionate tenderness. He fell completely under her spell, forgetting not only his quest but even his native land. The White Cat was, however, very aware of the passage of time and, just before the prince was due to return home, she reminded him of his search for the little dog. She presented the prince with an acorn in which was hidden a dog even more beautiful than the dog-star, and she lent him the wooden horse so he would not be late.

When he returned home, the youngest son easily won the contest to succeed his father, but the king, who was reluctant to give up his crown, decided to test his sons' courage and ingenuity a second time. His new demand was for a piece of cloth so fine that it would pass through the eye of a needle.

The youngest son remounted his wooden horse, and set out at full speed to the palace of the White Cat. The cat was highly delighted at his return, and he told her the nature of his second task. Another year slipped by as quickly as the first. Anything the prince wished for was immediately provided by the hands. The White Cat regaled him with a thousand different entertainments, and he enjoyed every minute that he spent in her company. He often asked her how it was that she could speak, and how she had come to be so very wise and talented. But she replied that she was not free to answer his questions, and that he must be content with the affectionate interest she took in all that concerned him.

When the second year was over and the prince had once

13. Preparations for the White Cat's hunt *p. 61*

14a. Celtic churchyard cross with cats carved on base

14b. Detail *p. 67*

more to leave, he found in the courtyard a golden carriage and four white horses harnessed with flame-coloured velvet studded with diamonds. There was also an escort of a thousand bodyguárds, and a hundred coaches, each drawn by eight horses and filled with noblemen. The livery of all this cavalcade bore an embroidered portrait of the White Cat. She told the prince that she hoped that if he returned to the king in splendour, all this magnificence would impress his royal father sufficiently to make him bestow the crown on his youngest son. As the procession was leaving the White Cat gave the prince a walnut, which she told him to crack in the king's presence, for in it he would find the fine cloth.

When the prince returned, and his father and brothers were rendered speechless by his magnificence, he took out the walnut and cracked it in front of them. Instead of the piece of cloth he had anticipated, however, inside it he found only a hazel nut. Cracking this nut, he found a cherry-stone; the cherry stone was filled with its kernel, the kernel with a grain of wheat, and the wheat with a millet-seed. In the face of his father's and brothers' jeering, the prince began to have doubts, and he muttered, "White Cat, thou hast fooled me." Immediately he said these words, he felt a cat's claw scratch his hand and draw blood. Then, opening the millet-seed, he drew out a piece of cloth four hundred ells in length, decorated with all the birds, beasts, fishes, trees, fruits and plants of the earth, with the sun, moon, stars and planets of the sky, and with portraits of all the kings and their subjects that had ever lived. The cloth was passed through the needle six times and, since there was nothing comparable to it in the universe, the king and his elder sons had to acknowledge that the young prince was again victorious.

The third and final test set by the king was that the three sons should travel for a third year in search of a maiden, and the one who returned with the most beautiful woman of all should marry her and be crowned on his wedding-day.

So, once again, the youngest son returned to the White Cat, who had so generously helped him to fulfil his other tasks. He found her seated on a Persian carpet under a gold pavilion, eagerly awaiting his arrival. He accompanied her to a terrace overlooking the sea, where they watched a naval combat she had arranged for his entertainment between her cats and the rats of the country. The cats sailed on large pieces of cork, and the rats' navy consisted of egg-shells. The rats swam much better than the cats, but it was not long before the cat-admiral devoured the rat-general. The White Cat forbade the total destruction of the rats, since she did not want her cats living in a state of idleness. The prince passed this third year in the company of the White Cat – fishing, hunting and playing chess with her. On the evening before he was due to return to his father's court, she reminded him of his task and she told him that, since he had to take home the most beautiful princess in the world, the time had come for him to destroy the work of the fairies by cutting off her head and tail, and flinging them into the fire. The prince, who by now deeply loved the White Cat and was very grateful for all her help, found it almost impossible to carry out her instructions. He did everything he could to induce her to spare him this trial, but she assured him that she wanted to die by his hand.

The moment the prince had cut off the cat's head and tail and flung them into the fire, he beheld a miraculous transformation, for she was now revealed as a beautiful maiden. Lords and ladies appeared with cat-skins flung over their shoulders and, kneeling before the maiden, spoke of their delight that their queen was at last restored to her natural form. When she was alone again with the prince, she explained that she had not always been a white cat. Her father had ruled over six kingdoms, but he had left her in the care of fairies who had planned that she should marry a monkey. When she refused and tried to run away with a handsome lover, the fairies changed her and all her lords and ladies into cats. She could only be released from feline form by a prince who perfectly resembled the husband of whom she had been deprived and whose miniature was set in her bracelet. She had been aware of her companion's resemblance to her lover ever since the moment she first saw him.

So the prince took the beautiful maiden home to his father. She travelled in a rock of crystal ornamented with gold and rubies, which was placed in a glorious chariot drawn by horses shod with emeralds. When they reached the prince's home, the rock burst into thousands of pieces and the princess appeared like a sun that had been hidden by the clouds. She was crowned with flowers, and her hair fell down to her feet over a white, roseate-lined gown.

The king wholeheartedly acknowledged that, although the maidens brought home by the two elder sons were exceptionally beautiful, the White Cat-maiden outshone them all and deserved the crown. So the marriage was celebrated without further delay between the youngest son of the king and the beautiful maiden who had appeared to be a White Cat, and brought him so much help and happiness.

The Sacrifice

Cats love the fireside: they gaze into the fire till its warmth overcomes them with drowsiness. The hearth has often been looked upon as a place of transformation: it was the place where the ragged Cinderella (the Hearth-Cat) was changed into a princess, and where the White Cat became a shining queen.

In addition to the "purgatorial" fire which purifies and

transforms, there is also the fire that represents consciousness, the inner flame that burns in man's soul. Prayers were offered to the ancient goddesses of the domestic hearth who guarded the flame at the centre of the family, and the flame at the centre of Roman civilization was closely guarded by the priestesses of Vesta.

It may be because of the cat's reputation as guardian of the hearth that it was believed to protect houses against destruction by fire. On the other hand, according to Herodotus, cats have a strange compulsion to throw themselves into fires. He describes how, when a house caught fire, the Egyptians would take the precaution of tying up all cats in the vicinity. Sometimes, however, they would manage to escape and "cats. leaping over the heads and gliding between the legs of the bystanders, rushed into the flames as if impelled by divine agency to suicide". The Egyptians totally disregarded the destruction of their property in their efforts to rescue their sacred cats from the flames.

So, there are various aspects of the cat's close association with fire. Sometimes it guards the fire; sometimes it is transformed by the fire or is burnt in the fire; at other times, as in the case of the Celtic myth of Maeldune, it *is* the fire. In many mythologies fire is an attribute of the Divine Son. In an apocryphal gospel, Christ says, "He that is near to me is near the fire." Cats' eyes often seem on fire at night and Bastet (who was connected with Bes, whose name meant "fire") represented the "flaming eye" of the sun. To this extent she was identified with the royal asps, whose forked, flickering, pink tongues symbolized the penetrating rays of the sun. It will be recalled that the original eye was transformed into a cobra, and Bastet was sometimes identified with the serpent-goddess, Udot, who was also looked upon as the eye of Ra.

In so far as the cat was *other* than the fire, it was destined to be destroyed by it. It was as an incarnation of the god of the setting sun that the cat had to be sacrificed to Horus, the rising sun, for, ultimately, the sacrifice people make is always of a god to a god. As the head and tail of the White Cat had to be burnt, in order that the maiden should regain her natural form, so the solar cat had to be sacrificed in order that it should rise again and its worshippers be reborn.

The spiritual significance of such a ceremony was so manifest that, in later times, the pagan rite of cat-sacrifice had the full support of the Christian Church. At Aix, in Provence, on Corpus Christi the finest tom-cat in the country was chosen each year and wrapped in swaddling clothes like an infant. It was then exhibited in a beautiful shrine for public adoration, and people burnt incense, strewed flowers and bent low before this incarnation of the solar god. When the sun crossed the meridian, the fêted cat was placed in a wicker basket and thrown alive into a huge bonfire in the city square. During the sacrifice of "the dying god", priests sang anthems and when the ceremony was complete they marched off in solemn procession.

In the light-aspect of its nature, the cat has been found closely connected with virgin birth and with resurrection. It was believed to be immortal, a seer and a healer, and to dedicate much of its life to the help of mankind. The cat said to be born at the same moment as Christ is usually depicted with a cross-shaped marking on its back, and a Celtic churchyard-cross at Monasterboice, County Louth, in Ireland, has two cats sculptured on its base. (One of the cats is licking a newly-born kitten, while the other is disposing of a bird. Plate 14b.)

The devotees of the cat that emerged as a symbol of Christ knew that all they valued most had to die in order that new life and light could be born.

PART II

The Black Cat

To turn now to the cat that people "can't abide". Black cats are often felt to be uncanny, and some would say they are distinctly sinister.

The Circle

When a cat lies coiled at the fireside, it gives one a sense of repose and completion, and the circle that it forms is a symbol of eternity. But there is such a thing as a vicious circle, and it is this unpleasant aspect of its symbolism that is represented by a cat lying curled up when it is black.

We have already noted that cats and snakes share (in their lighter aspects) certain physical habits, and certain associations in myth and folklore. Plate 17 shows the bronze figure of a sacred Egyptian cat whose head is crowned by a coiled serpent. But snakes are poisonous, and cats hiss and spit, and the image of the black cat and that of the dark serpent can be interchangeable.

Many mythologies tell of a cosmic serpent which lies encircling the whole world, holding its tail in its mouth. This all-powerful being is hermaphroditic, self-begetting, and has no beginning or end. It is static and eternal, and is found in widely differing cultures. The Babylonians called it "Tiamat", the Hebrews called it "Leviathan", and sometimes this image of the coiled serpent merges with the image of the coiled cat.

In Teutonic myth the earth was called *Midgard*, because it existed midway between heaven and hell. (In this case an account is given of how the monster was born and met its end, but as both the preceding and superseding Nordic gods had their serpents, there is still a sense in which it was "static and eternal".)

The Midgard Serpent was the offspring of Loki, the Devil, and of the Hag who was known as the "Mother of Evil". Odin, father of the gods, who lived in the celestial city of Asgard, discovered early on, by means of divination, that this young monster was being reared in the nether regions with the express purpose of bringing disaster to the gods. If it was not overcome, Thor, the mighty god of thunder, would be killed by it. This information flung Odin into a raging fury and he commanded that the young serpent should be captured and brought to him immediately. Finding it was already immensely long and very ferocious, he seized the creature and hurled it over the walls of Asgard. Its weight was, unfortunately, so great that, instead of disappearing over the edge of the world as the indignant god intended, it fell short into the depths of the ocean. Lying on the slimy ocean-bed, the serpent grew and grew till eventually it completely encircled Midgard and was able to grasp its own tail.

Thor, however, could never feel really safe so long as the Midgard Serpent was alive, and he made several attempts to kill it, but always came off much the worse for wear.

One day, the god of thunder decided to make a journey into the land of the frost-giants, whose icy blasts were blighting the fields of Midgard. He was accompanied on this escapade by

Loki and, after overcoming many obstacles, they came to an ice-castle where they found the king of the frost-giants enthroned. After an extremely chilly welcome, the king tauntingly invited Thor to prove his strength. A huge grey cat leapt forward and sat before the throne, and the king challenged the god of thunder to lift it off the floor. Thor confidently approached the cat and grasped it firmly, placing his hands under its belly. But when he tried to lift it up, the animal bent its great back and, although the god used all the strength he could muster, he only succeeded in lifting one of its paws off the floor. The king added to Thor's humiliation by remarking that the god appeared a puny weakling compared with his own race of giants.

In all the trials of his strength and skill, Thor dismally failed. But when, next day, he was taking leave of the frost-giants, their king pointedly asked him if he felt satisfied with his visit. The god confessed that he had been covered with shame, and that what caused him the greatest anguish was that he should have been dubbed a man of little account. The giant then had the grace to admit that Thor had only failed because he had been grossly deceived, and that in fact the giants had the greatest respect for the thunder-god's power and skill. The king of the frost-giants explained how, when Thor had struggled with the great cat, they had all marvelled at his strength and were terrified when they saw him lift a single paw off the floor; for the cat, he said, was none other than the Midgard Serpent which encircled the earth.

A description of the final death-struggle between Thor and the serpent, during the cataclysmic battle at the Twilight of the Gods, brings home to one the full power and horror of this monster who had taken the form of a cat. We find the serpent writhing in rage on the ocean's bed, so that waves as high as mountains billow over the shores of the earth. As it rears its shaggy head out of the sea, it breathes out fire and, faced with the god of thunder, it coils and uncoils, pouring floods of venom over him and suffocating him with its poisonous breath.

The images of the encircling serpent and the cat are again closely associated in a Christian myth found in the Coptic apocryphal gospel, *Pistis Sophia*. In this myth, Jesus describes to the Virgin Mary how "the outer darkness is a great serpent, the tail of which is in its mouth, and it is outside the whole world, and surroundeth the whole world". In this serpent of darkness, there are twelve halls in which severe punishment is inflicted, and there are governors in charge of each hall. The governor of the second judgement hall, we are told, "hath as his true face the face of a cat", and there are seven cat-faced governors in charge of the eleventh hall. So it is almost as if the image of hell were split into two, with the serpent representing its passive, engulfing aspect and the cat playing the role of its vengeful executive.

It is possible, of course, that these cat-faced governors were forms of the pre-Christian god, Osiris – the father of Bastet – who was closely associated with the goddess of law and justice. As Ruler of the Dead, Osiris is often portrayed holding a royal whip with nine lashes. Perhaps our comparatively modern cat-o'-nine-tails derives from the practices of these torturing officials of the Coptic hell.

The Devourer

In life the cat and the snake fight each other; and, although the images of the cat and serpent sometimes overlap, they more often stand in opposition. When the shining, celestial cat of the sun-god, Ra, fought the advancing darkness of the night, the devourer took the form of a serpent. But the snake can also be a symbol of light and life; and, when the setting sun took the form of the fiery asp, then it was the cat who incarnated darkness, chaos and death. The cosmic cat in its dark, demonic aspect was, like the Coptic serpent of hell, the devourer of all that had form.

Devourers of the magnitude of the encircling serpent, or of the cat that swallowed the sun, are always hermaphroditic. (They have not got as far as sorting out themselves into male and female.) But since the sun, with its penetrating rays, is essentially a symbol of the masculine principle, it was the passive, engulfing aspect of the cat that was emphasized in this context, and she emerged as a symbol of the darker aspect of femininity.

So the black cat took its place among the great devouring goddesses (sometimes shown as bearded to remind us that they are not wholly feminine) that are to be found in most mythologies. She joined the ranks of those female deities who played cat-and-mouse with the handsome young fertility-gods of the spring, loving, castrating, and finally slaying them. Although the sun-goddess, Freya, whose chariot was drawn by a lively pair of cats, primarily represented fruitfulness, she also led the Valkyries to the battlefields, claiming from Odin her right to choose men destined to be devoured by death. As a death-goddess she was known in Germany as Hel, and she represented there the destructiveness of the winter months.

As a vehicle of the German goddess, Hel, or of the Greek goddess, Hecate, the black cat was considered by many people to be an omen of death. There appears to be no end to the stories told of black phantom-cats that have been seen by dying people, or by their relatives, when death is imminent. Typical is one of a woman who was nursing her sick grandfather. As she left his room one night and was walking down a corridor, a strange black cat appeared and fled past her. She ran after it but, in spite of searching the whole house, was unable to find any trace of the animal. Her mother later confessed that she also had seen a strange cat walking round the invalid's bed that evening, but when she had tried to find the cat it seemed to have vanished into thin air. The following day the grandfather died.

Germans believed that if a black cat jumped onto the bed of someone who was ill it foretold his approaching death. In Normandy it was believed that, if a black cat crossed your path in moonlight, you would probably die from an epidemic within the year, while to the Chinese a black cat was an omen of sickness and poverty.

Among the less endearing habits of cats is the way in which they maim and destroy birds and mice. The bird, which spends its days in sunlit skies, is a symbol of the life of soaring spirit. The mosaic that was found in the ruins of Pompeii, depicting a bright-eyed cat pouncing on a bird (Plate 18), powerfully expresses this dark aspect of the cat, seen as a feminine destroyer of male spirituality.

Similarly, although mice are usually demonic, they also have often represented the soul, and in Teutonic folklore they were considered to be the souls of the dead. The mouse was sacred to the Greek sun-god, Apollo, whose priests kept white mice, which had their holes under Apollo's altar and were daily fed as a religious rite. It is said that the cat was the only animal not allowed to attend the Buddha's funeral, for it had disgraced itself by killing the rat that had been sent to fetch medicine to heal him. (Snakes also feed on rodents, and the cat and poisonous viper had apparently distinguished themselves by failing to weep when the Buddha died.) When, in mythology, the cat is black and evil, the mice are usually

white and numinous; when, on the contrary, the cat is white
and a symbol of spirituality, then the mice appear as black and
demonic.

The Witch

The walk of a cat is almost inaudible and, if, on a moonless
night, we meet a black cat stealthily prowling through the
engulfing darkness, it seems almost to incarnate the gloom.
The dark side of the moon is personified in a witch (who may
be male but is usually female), and there is an archaic myth
which gives an account of her origin.

Before all creation, there existed a goddess of darkness
called Diana. At the beginning, all things were one in her
(as they were in the coiled serpent or cat), but she later
divided herself into male and female, and into darkness and
light. The light-half of Diana was her brother, Lucifer; and
the goddess of darkness loved and desired the god of light.
But Lucifer did not want to be possessed by darkness and,
although Diana pursued him every night, he repulsed her
immodest advances. Diana eventually discovered, however,
that Lucifer had a beautiful fairy-cat which always slept
beside him. She persuaded this cat to change places with her
one night and, from the union of the goddess of darkness with
the god of light, there was born a daughter, Aradia. Aradia
was named the first of the witches, and Diana sent her to the
earth to teach human beings the art of witchcraft. That was
the beginning of black magic, and it was taught in the name
of Diana, Queen of the Witches, who had "changed places"
with a beautiful fairy-cat.

Gods of an earlier religion become demons in the cult that
supersedes it; thus, with the rise of Christianity, priestesses

of the moon-goddesses came to be regarded as witches. People who had previously worshipped the fruitful Freya now banished her to the barren mountain-tops, and they looked upon her divine cats as the demonic steeds which bore the witches aloft. As degenerate survivors of the moon's priestesses, the witches had lunar powers within their control. The moon was believed to have power over the human body and mind, over the fertility of animals and crops and, above all, over weather conditions and the tides.

The cat has become part of sailors' lives at sea. To hear them talk you would think they were obsessed with cats, for in several languages the word for "cat" has a nautical connotation. In English, a small, single-masted boat is known as a "cat-boat", and its rigging is the "cat-rig". The beam used for carrying the anchor is called the "cat-head", and hanging the anchor on the cat-head is known as "catting the anchor". There is also a short rope or iron cramp which is called a "catharpin".

Sailors will draw omens from the behaviour of their cats. They will "see how the cat jumps" (or which way the wind blows), and mewing cats or frolicking cats on board are believed to presage a gale. "Cat's-paw" is the name they give to a light breeze which ripples the water during a calm, and indicates an approaching squall. In Scotland, a cat scratching table- or chair-legs is said to be "raising wind". In Lapland, people look to their cats for the weather forecast before setting out on a journey.

It is true, of course, that cats are sensitive to changes of atmosphere, and become acutely nervous and restless before a storm. (There is a Slavic belief that in thunderstorms cats' bodies are inhabited by devils. At every clap of thunder the angels pray to God, and the devils hidden in cats mock them. It is wise to clear cats out of the house during thunderstorms for, in order to drive the devils out of cats, angels throw down shafts of lightning which could easily set the house on fire.) But the nautical cats had a lot to answer for. Although they were only supposed to be ordinary animals who happened to have foreknowledge of bad weather, their owners half-believed that they created it. In Ireland, as soon as storms began to rise, all available cats were seized and placed under a metal pot, where they were held until they used their power to bring about a calm. Sailors knew that witches often took feline form and, as lunar manipulators of the tides and weather, had the power to raise tempestuous seas. Shakespeare refers, in *The Tempest*, to:

> A witch; and one so strong
> She could control the moon – make flows and ebbs.

(It was said that information about flows and ebbs could be elicited from cats' eyes, for the slits were vertical at the flood, and horizontal when the tide was ebbing.)

There is a seventeenth-century print, by a Polish engraver, which shows witches leaving a Sabbat assembly on their broomsticks, flying off, we are told, "to raise storms and tempests". A fifteenth-century engraving shows a witch stirring up a terrible storm, and making a ship founder by emptying her cauldron into the sea. Another depicts a sailor buying winds from a sorcerer. The sorcerer is standing on a rock jutting out into the sea and is carrying a knotted rope. Apparently winds are tied up in the three knots, and when the navigator undoes them he may expect, from the first knot, a gentle south-westerly wind; from the second knot, a strong northerly wind; and from the third knot, a roaring tempest.

There is a Scottish legend which tells how a Spanish king sent a war vessel to Mull, with instructions to avenge the murder of his daughter by a Scottish witch. The witches of

Mull were furious and, taking the shape of cats, they gathered together on the shrouds of the Spanish ship, determined to sink it. The captain, however, knew something of the art of magic, and was able to counteract their spells. So the witches called on the power of their Highland queen, and she instantly appeared on top of the mast in the form of a gigantic black cat. This put paid to the puny efforts of the captain, for the witches' queen had only just begun to chant one of her spells when the vessel sank like a stone to the bottom of the sea.

Witches would sail through, or under, tempestuous seas in sieves, using their brooms as oars. The sieve was used for divination, and was one of the implements of magic found in any witch's kitchen. It was often depicted on gnostic gems for, before moon-worship came to be despised, it was an emblem of Isis, the white goddess of the calm seas.

A legend from the Isle of Skye tells of a married woman who disappeared from home every night. One evening her anxious husband decided to follow her and, to his astonishment, he watched his wife transform herself into a sleek, black cat and, in the name of the Devil, go to sea in a sieve along with seven other black cats. Horror-stricken, the husband invoked the Trinity, and this promptly upset the sieve and drowned all the witches.

But storm-raising cats were not always witches; they were sometimes quite ordinary cats which were used by sorcerers as instruments of black magic. A Scottish sorcerer was seen leaping over hedges and ditches in pursuit of cats. On trial, he stated that Satan needed all the cats that his servants could bring him since he was unable, without their help, to raise storms or wreck ships.

Highland witches could raise a storm by drawing a cat through a fire, and by christening a cat and casting it into the sea. British law-courts have recorded many cases where it was claimed that witches were responsible for the destruction of ships. An account of the trial of Agnes Sampson, one of the most famous of Scottish witches, includes a description of such a rite involving a cat.

Agnes was accused of trying to shipwreck King James and Queen Anne on their journey home from Denmark. This ambitious witch was "brought to Haliriud-House, before the king's majestie, and sundry other of the nobilitie of Scotland, where she was straytly examined." But the court was quite unable to persuade her to confess anything, for she "stoode stiffely in the deniall of all that was layde to her charge". So Agnes was taken off to prison and tortured until she was prepared to talk. She was then brought again before the king's court, and this time she made her confession.

On All-Hallows' Even, she said, she was one of two hundred witches who went to sea in sieves which were well stocked with flagons of wine. They drank and made merry, until they came to a kirk in Lowthian. Here they disembarked and continued their jollifications, singing and wildly dancing around in circles.

At the time when the king was in Denmark, Agnes, with her same two hundred companions, "tooke a cat and christened it, and afterwards bounde to each part of that cat the cheefest parte of a dead man and severall joyntes of his bodie; and in the night following, the saide cat was convayed into the middest of the sea by all those witches, sayling in their riddles or cives". They left the cat near the town of Leith. Then, sure enough, "there did arise such a tempest in the sea as a greater hath not bene seene", and this resulted in the foundering of a ship making for Leith, which was laden with jewels and riches to be presented to the new Queen of Scotland. Agnes further confessed, that "the said christened cat was the cause that the kinges majesties shippe, at his comming forth

15. The "Sleeping Cat" talisman *p. 49*

16. The "Beckoning Cat" charm *p. 53*

17. Egyptian sacred cat crowned with coiled snake *p. 68*

of Denmarke, had a contrarie winde to the rest of his shippes then being in his companie". And she admitted that the king only got home safely because his faith had been stronger than the will of the witches.

As early as the end of the seventh century, English ecclesiastical law was directed against those who, by invoking fiends, caused storms. A hundred years later Charlemagne decreed the death penalty against those who, by means of the Devil, disturbed the air and excited tempests. In 1484 Pope Innocent VIII explicitly charged sorcerers with these practices.

It was not only in order to raise tempests, however, that witches turned themselves into cats. The moon is always changing her form, and shape-shifting is one of the powers attributed to the devotees of her darker side.

Stories told of women in feline form were accepted in sixteenth-century ecclesiastical courts as evidence of witchcraft. Aberdeen witches were accused of having assumed the likeness of cats in order to celebrate their orgies undisturbed around the Fish Cross. Witch-cats apparently talked with human voices, but often in an unknown language.

A case was reported of a German witch who, sentenced to be burnt at the stake, defied the judge, laughed at the executioner and mocked the priest with blasphemies. The wood was set alight, her body was enveloped with smoke and the priest was kneeling in prayer when, with a wild exultant screech, a black cat leapt out of the flames – and the witch, disappearing among the crowds, had escaped.

Members of a primitive Bengali tribe believe that some women have the power to change their souls into black cats, and that any wound or mutilation inflicted on the cats will be suffered by the women. (They say that such cats are easily recognized by their peculiar way of mewing.)

There are many European stories of witches being identified by wounds inflicted on cats. Typical is the case of a Scottish laird, who noticed that his wine was mysteriously diminishing. Suspecting that his loss was due to witchcraft, he armed himself with a sword one night and descended to the cellars. Immediately, the laird was surrounded by black cats. Laying about him with his sword, he soon cleared the cellar of them all, but not without mutilating one of them. Next day an old woman in the village, who had the reputation of being a witch, was found in bed with one of her legs off.

A sixteenth-century French political writer tells how the witches of Vernon were reputed to assemble in an old ruined castle in the form of black cats. Four foolhardy men arranged to spend the night in the notorious castle, and found themselves assailed on all sides by hundreds of witch-cats, who killed one of the men and severely wounded the other three. The men managed, however, to leave their mark on the cats, and the next day a number of old women in the neighbourhood were found bleeding and mutilated in their beds.

There is also the story of a labourer of Strasbourg who found himself in an embarrassing position. He was walking down the main street one night when he was suddenly attacked by three huge cats. Hitting out at them in self-defence, he damaged them. Shortly afterwards he was arrested on a charge of maltreating three well-known ladies of the town. He vigorously denied the accusation but, when the ladies in question were medically examined, they were found to be suffering from the wounds he had inflicted on the cats.

A more homely story tells of a French woman who was cooking an omelet one day when a black cat strolled into her cottage and sat on the hearth. After watching the woman attentively for a few minutes, the cat said, "It is done. Turn it over." In her indignation at being ordered about by a cat, the woman flung the half-cooked eggs at its head. Next morning she saw a deep red burn on the cheek of a malicious neighbour.

The Basques claimed, at the end of the nineteenth century, that witches still appeared in the shape of black cats. They tell how, at midnight, a farmer chopped off an ear of a black cat which was bewitching his cattle. Next morning he found on the ground a woman's ear which, he swore, still had a ring dangling from it.

There were, however, means of dealing with assaulting witch-cats in spite of the fact that no bolts or bars excluded them. At the trial of a witch called Isobel Grierson, who was burnt at the stake in 1607, she was accused of two offences. On one occasion, it was declared, she assumed cat form and, accompanied not only by a rabble of cats but also by the Devil himself in the form of a black man, she broke into the house of one Adam Clark. We are not given details of what happened, except that the black man seized the maid and dragged her down to the ground by her hair! On an occasion when Isobel made a similar visit to a couple in the same town, the witch-cat sprang and landed on the man's wife. But this time she was recognized, and when she was called by her name she immediately vanished. It is also said that if the Devil hears pronounced the name of Jesus, he will run away in the form of a black cat.

At the trial of Susanna Martin for witchcraft in 1692, a man testified that, when she had previously been prosecuted in court for being a witch, he had stated that he believed she was in fact one, and she had indignantly shouted threats against him. The following night, as the man lay in bed, a huge cat appeared at his window, entered and flew at his throat. It lay on his chest, he said, for a considerable time, and nearly killed him. Eventually, when he had gathered his wits, he cried out, "Avoid, thou she-devil, in the name of God the Father, the Son, and the Holy Ghost," at which the cat immediately leapt to the floor and flew out of the window. (We have already seen how witches could be drowned by the naming of the Trinity.)

There is also the story of the Norwegian mill which had twice been burnt to the ground on Whitsun Eve. The third year, a travelling tailor, hearing of the local suspicions, offered to keep watch overnight. His method of dealing with witches was to chalk a circle on the floor with the Lord's Prayer written round it. At midnight, a troop of cats crept stealthily in carrying a great pot of pitch, which they hung in the fireplace, lighting logs beneath it. Soon the pitch bubbled and seethed and the cats swung the pot back and forth, doing their utmost to overturn it. The tailor, from his position of safety, shouted at the cats and, when their leader tried to pull him outside the magic circle, he cut off its paw with his knife, and they all fled howling into the night. Next morning, the mill was still standing, but the miller's wife was ill in bed, suffering from an amputated hand.

A Scottish witch confessed that, when she and others changed themselves into cats and tried to steal into farmhouses at night, they could not get in where the farms were "fenced against them by prayer and charms". (The power of Christianity does not, however, seem to have been infallible when confronted with witchcraft. A woodcutter of Brittany once saw thirteen cats "dancing in sacrilegious glee" round a wayside cross. And when a charcoal-burner in the Black Forest came upon three cats sitting in the moonlight by his kiln, a cord he wore round his neck snapped, and the saint's relic it held fell to the ground. When he tried to pick it up he could not, for his arm hung helplessly by his side.)

Some people believed that witches were powerless in the

neighbourhood of a rowan tree, and that if you shook a branch of a rowan at witch-cats they would vanish. The following poem, written in 1830, refers to the use of rowan to keep black cats (batrons) away from children's cradles:

> How the auld uncanny matrons
> Grew whiles a hare, a dog, or batrons,
> To get their will a' carles sleepan,
> Wha hae nae staulks o' rauntree keepan,
> Ty'd round them when they ride or sail,
> Or sew't wi' care in their sark-tail.

Little is known of the means by which a woman is transformed into a cat. A Scottish witch on trial said that when, on one occasion, the coven she belonged to assembled in their own forms to work evil spells, they were accompanied by the Devil, who turned them into cats by shaking his hands above their heads.

A French witch confessed that she was in the habit of rubbing her body over with black ointment, which transformed her into a cat and enabled her to steal unobserved through the darkness. There is a Greek myth, told by Ovid, of a woman who was transformed into a cat. This is the story of Galinthias, the loyal servant of the Princess Alcmene. Alcmene was about to be delivered of Heracles, but Hera, queen of heaven, was furious because Zeus, her husband, was the father of this child, and she was doing everything she could to prevent the birth. Galinthias then played a trick on Hera, which allowed her mistress to give birth to the young hero. As a result, the outraged Hera changed Galinthias into a cat and banished her to the underworld, where she became a priestess of Hecate, queen of the witches and the goddess of death.

At Isobel Gowdrie's trial in 1662, this queen of Scottish

witches, gave an explicit account of her ritual transformation
by the use of magical words. The formula she used to change
herself into a cat had to be repeated three times:

> I shall goe intill ane catt,
> With sorrow, and sych, and a blak shott;
> And I sall goe in the Divellis nam,
> Ay quhill I com hom againe.

("Home again" here means "to my own shape".)
She described how she and her coven rambled, in the form of
cats, through the countryside, eating, drinking and squander-
ing their neighbours' goods. They returned to human form by
use of this spell:

> Catt, catt, God send thee a blak shott.
> I am in a cattis liknes just now,
> Bot I sal be in a womanis liknes ewin now.
> Catt, catt, God send thee a blak shott.

(According to Baldwin's book, *Beware of the Cat*, which was
published in 1584, "It was permitted to a witch to take on her
catte's body nine times.")

Members of Isobel Gowdrie's coven could turn one another
into cats. If a witch in feline form met one who was not
transformed, and greeted her: "The Devil speed thee, go thou
with me," the second witch would immediately take the shape
of a cat, and they would make off together.

A Japanese legend tells of a witch who haunted Okabe, a
posting station on the Tokaido road. She lived in a hut under
a group of pines near the temple, and her great delight was to
assume the form of a cat and lie in wait to frighten young
women visiting the temple. Eventually, however, the witch's
evil turned back on her, transforming her into the "cat-stone"
still to be seen there. Plate *19* shows a scene from a Japanese

play, performed in 1835, on the subject of the Tokaido station, where the Okabe witch is being transformed into a cat.

The Waternish "Cat's Cairn" in Scotland commemorates the tragic fate of a boy who accidentally came upon three old village women in the act of transforming themselves into black cats. He was sworn to secrecy by them, but his mother succeeded in persuading him to tell her what had happened. It was not long before the witch-cats took their revenge, for the cairn, which is crowned by a long, sharp stone resembling a huge claw, marks the spot where the boy was found clawed to death.

The Familiar

Due to the witch's propensity for shape-shifting, her image and that of her cat often merge, so that the two are indistinguishable. But witches and cats are also two separate beings, and in so far as they are separate the black cat is the witch's familiar.

The cat's blackness, unearthly wailings and natural nocturnal habits having intimately associated it with witches, the horror of the activities for which it is blamed is almost boundless. People feared the darkness and void of the moonless night. Their imagination tended to fill it with all that they found most frightening and most repulsive, and this became incarnated in the witch and her cat. Much doubt has, of course, been thrown on the evidence given at the sixteenth-century witch-trials and to be found in contemporary writings on the subject of witchcraft and black magic generally. But, since our concern is entirely with people's *beliefs*, whether or not the claims made were objectively true is not important for the purpose of this investigation. There is no doubt whatever that they truly expressed what people believed.

We have explored the whole field of the cat's reputation as a goddess of shining purity. Such a powerful light throws a very deep shadow, and, if we are to get a true picture of what this animal has, as a whole, meant to people, it is necessary to plumb the depths of her dark reputation however distasteful it may prove to be.

All witches had their feline spirits which accompanied them on their nightly flights. Such women, we are told, grew an "unnatural nipple" with which they suckled their familiars. (The blood-sucking cat-familiar must not be confused with the cat-vampire, for witches taught and encouraged their familiars to drink their blood in order to create and strengthen a psychic bond between them.)

In 1579, a witch tried at Windsor confessed to possessing a spirit in the shape of a black cat, "whereby she is aided in her witchcrafte, and she daiely feedeth it with Milke, mingled with her owne bloud". At another trial held in Essex a few years later, evidence was given of a cat-familiar who would come to the witch during the night "and suckle bloud of her upon her armes and other places of her body".

The Devil, who favoured the form of a black cat, appeared to a Suffolk witch and, she confessed, "sucketh of a Tett and hath drawn bloud". The only evidence we have of what this psychic suckling felt like was given by a Somerset witch who stated that, when her cat-familiar suckled her, she was usually in a trance.

Sometimes witches would offer blood to their familiars by pricking themselves. When, in 1646, the witches of Huntingdonshire were tried, one woman explained how she had originally been given a cat by a witch and told that, if she would deny God "and affirme the same by her bloud, then whomsoever she cursed, and sent the Cat unto them, they should dye shortly after". This she had agreed to do and, pricking her finger with a thorn, had given it to the cat to lick.

Once cat and witch were thus intimately united, the cat to some extent shared the witch's powers, so anything that we learn about witches has its bearing on the lives of their cat-familiars. Witches obtained their supernatural powers through making a pact with the Devil. In addition to their ability to become invisible, to fly and to raise storms at sea, witches could, by incantation, summon the Devil and evil spirits of all shapes and kinds, and the necromancers raised the dead.

In Spain, necromancy was taught in deep caverns, the most famous of which were found in Toledo and Seville. The witch would stand in a churchyard, using a wand to trace round herself round a circle which she filled with crosses, anchors and magical words. A necromantic bell would sometimes be used to evoke the dead. An eighteenth-century manuscript contains an illustration of such a bell, showing the name "Adonai" inscribed on one side of the handle and on the other side the name "Jesus". Inscriptions to be found all over the bell include the word "Tetragrammaton", the date of birth of the person who is to use it, and the names of the seven planets. According to the instructions, the bell must be wrapped in a piece of green taffeta until the necromancer is ready to use it. She then puts the bell in the middle of a grave and leaves it there for seven days, after which she will be able to evoke the dead at will. The Witch of Endor was one of the most famous necromancers, for she is said to have raised the Prophet Samuel from his tomb. Witches and sorcerers would forgather in cemeteries. They needed dead men's bones for their charms, and they increased their supernatural powers by feasting on the corpses they had disinterred.

Witches could bring all kinds of misfortune on people, for a highly valued gift they received from the Devil was the power of revenge. They could lay waste the countryside, injuring cattle and ruining crops. They could cause affliction or death by breathing on people, or by the use of magical words in spells. Possessing the evil eye, they could kill by a glance or transform people into animals or into stone. They could stir up quarrels among friends, and blight people's lives with their philtres (which were made of such ingredients as the heart of a dove, the kidney of a hare and the womb of a swallow, all reduced to powder and mixed with the witch's blood). They could provoke epidemics, cause impotence, prevent conception, and dry up the milk of nursing mothers. They could bring agony and death on their enemies by the use of waxen images, whose hearts they pierced and exposed to heat until they slowly melted away.

Now, as the loyal servant of the witch, the cat-familiar took an active part in the perpetration of these nefarious deeds. One witch confessed that a cat had come one night to her cottage when she was cowering over her fire, nursing angry thoughts against a farmer's wife. This animal stayed with her for months, stealing out each night to obey her foul commands until there was hardly a woman in the village who had not suffered from its malignity. Another witch admitted that, whenever her cat carried out her wishes, she pricked her hand or face and allowed it to suck drops of her blood as a reward. Many witches were hanged on being convicted of sending a "wantoune cat" to work evil on people who had offended them.

A witch who nursed a venomous hatred of the Earl and Countess of Rutland was hanged at Lincoln in 1618 for having used her cat-familiar to deprive them of their children. In her confession, this terrible old woman explained how she had got hold of a glove belonging to the son and heir, soaked it in scalding water, pricked it with pins and, rubbing it on the body of her black cat, bade her familiar fly off and carry out her will. The boy became ill immediately and was racked by pain until he died. The younger son was similarly bewitched, and passed away miserably in his mother's arms. Not content with murdering the Rutlands' children, the witch obtained feathers from the Countess's bed and, by rubbing them on the belly of her cat-familiar, ensured that the woman she had rendered childless would never again be capable of giving birth to a live baby.

One cat-familiar caused mortal illness by blowing on a child; another was used to prevent Christians from reading the Bible; a third was employed to destroy three hogs and a cow, which belonged to a farmer who had incurred the hatred of the witch.

Hungarians believed that most cats became witches between the ages of seven and twelve years. It was possible, however, to deliver the cat from the witch by making an incision on its skin in the form of a cross.

The heart of the witches' existence as a corporate society lay in their frequent gatherings, known as Sabbats. These assemblies were connected with the phases of the moon, and their practices were a degenerate form of religious rites previously performed by priestesses of the moon-goddess. The covens met on mountain-tops, at cross-roads or in caves, under the presidency of the Devil.

Some say that the Sabbat was held four times a year, coinciding with the Christian festivals. Others maintain that witches met much more frequently, forgathering whenever they were so commanded by the Devil. Sorcerers and witches had a little blue mark imprinted on hidden parts of their bodies, and an uncomfortable tingling in this spot warned them when their attendance at the Sabbat was required.

Much information about the ritual preparations made for Sabbats is available from the many engravings on the subject produced during the sixteenth century. A typical scene of a witch's kitchen will show a background littered with broomsticks, forks, bones, pots of unguent, drugs, a book of magic, and a sieve, and it will be enlivened with such animals as owls, snakes, toads and bats. In the foreground a skull will probably be seen lying in the centre of a circle full of cabbalistic signs, which is traced on the floor. The old witches are portrayed as hideous hags, the others as beautiful young women. The ancient ones will be blowing a fire, stirring the contents of a large cauldron, or disappearing up a chimney on a broomstick. Witches achieved their power to fly by anointing their bodies with unguent, and in the centre of many of these prints an old woman can be seen rubbing grease over the body of a young witch, with one or several black cat-familiars in attendance.

Witches usually attended the Sabbats naked, and Plate 20 shows four of them preparing for their departure. An old witch is already off among the clouds, mounted on a fork and followed by a flying goat. Another witch has a cat in her arms, which she probably intends to use as a means of transportation. The other two are engaged in preparing the unguent, grinding the drugs to powder in a little cauldron.

The preparation of the ointment was guarded as a precious secret. It was made from the fat of unbaptized children, and often included soot, and the blood of lapwings and bats. The witches would rub it all over themselves, until their bodies were red and their pores had absorbed it all. By this means, we are told, "on a moonlight night they seeme to be carried in the aire". Sometimes the unguent was presented to the witches by the Devil himself. (Five women, charged with witchcraft in 1460, described how the Devil had made them such a gift, and how, whenever they wanted to go to the Sabbats, they anointed a wooden rod and their hands with it. They explained how "putting this small rod between their legs, straightway they flew where they wished to be", and that the Devil guided them over towns, woods and waters, to the place of assembly.)

In the foreground of Plate 20, we find a cat-familiar studying the inevitable "Black Book", the Bible of the witches. It contained the secret of how to become invisible, magical formulae used for the evocation of demons, and spells which would produce poisons and philtres.

When at last the witches were ready to leave, they mounted either black flying-cats, or goats, or sometimes they flew off on broomsticks or forks. A carving on a fourteenth-century door in Lyons cathedral depicts a witch on her way to a Sabbat. She is riding naked on a flying goat, holding onto one of its horns with her right hand, while in her left hand she clutches a black cat, which she appears to be whirling around the goat's head. In 1673, a member of a Northumbrian coven described how she had herself been ridden. One night, she claimed, a witch appeared in the form of a grey cat with a bridle hanging from its foot. It breathed on her, struck her unconscious, bridled her and, in the name of the Devil, rode her to the Sabbat meeting.

Once the witches felt themselves summoned to the Sabbat, nothing would prevent their going. A man who discovered his wife rubbing herself all over with unguent tied her to the bed with ropes, but she changed into a bat and flew off up the chimney. More remarkable still is the tale of a witch who was fortunate enough to have her jar of ointment with her when she stood before the Inquisition in Navarre. How she was able to apply it is not divulged, but she succeeded in changing

herself into an owl, and flew off to the Sabbat under the very
eyes of the judges.

The Devil

The Sabbats were held in the depth of the night, and were
presided over by the Devil in the form of a black cat, or sometimes of a goat or a black man. (According to evidence
obtained at witch-trials, Satan took the form of a black cat
on a thousand occasions, of a goat two hundred and fifty times,
and appeared only sixty times as a black man.) In Plate 21,
where a witch is teaching a novice to levitate, the Devil is
incarnated as a goat, while the two cat-familiars may be taken
as representing aspects of both the Devil and the witch. One
place where Sabbats were held was the Cats' Field (Prat des
Gats) near Sabarat, where a dolmen was believed to be
inhabited by a witch. Her name, *Matèbe*, reminds one of
matou, a tom-cat. Descriptions of the Sabbat ceremonies are,
although unsavoury, quite fascinating, for they consist of
elements taken from Christian ritual, and also from ancient
white fertility rites – only everything in them is reversed.

When the host of witches and sorcerers had flown in, they
started by paying homage to the enthroned Devil. They made
offerings to him of unbaptized children, they renewed their
oaths of fidelity and obedience to him, and each in turn filed
past him to kiss his posterior. (Some witches claimed that he
kept a second face under his tail!) They would then celebrate
Black Mass, lighting their black candles from the torch on the
Devil's head and turning their backs to the altar. Eventually
they all settled down to the Sabbat feast, at which, we are
told, would be served the flesh of hanged men, the hearts of
unbaptized children and a variety of unclean animals.

Having eaten their fill, the witches would render accounts to the Devil of the evil they had done since the last assembly, and they would receive instructions from him as to how they were expected to proceed. The most popular witches were those who had caused the greatest number of deaths, cast most spells of illness on people and cattle, and spoilt the most fruit and grain. Those who had behaved more humanely were hissed and derided by the others, and were beaten and maltreated by the Devil.

Sometimes hail was ritually produced at the Sabbats with the intention of ruining the crops. Sorcerers would beat water with a wand, then throw into it a powder which the Devil gave to them. This caused a cloud to rise up from the water which afterwards turned into hail. (It is interesting to note that the Languedoc form of the Christian St Agatha's name was *Santo Gato* – St Cat. She was closely associated with thunderstorms, and on her feast-day peasants rang church-bells in all the villages to ward off hail which it was believed was "made" then. When the saint wished to punish women who insulted her by working on her feast-day, she chose to appear in the form of an angry cat. This seems to be a case in which black and white magic merge.)

It was during Sabbats that novices made pacts with the Devil. When he baptized them they had to trample on the Cross, and he gave them a Black Book in exchange for the Gospels. He marked them, sometimes leaving the imprint of his claw under their left eyelids. In return for their oaths, he promised to help and protect them, and gave them familiars of their own. (In 1669, three hundred Swedish children – boys and girls aged between six and sixteen – were said to have been drawn to Sabbat meetings and enrolled in Satan's ranks. They confessed to receiving from the Devil "a beast about the bigness and shape of a young cat". These animals were apparently known as "carriers", and their duty was to steal butter, cheese, milk and bacon, and bring the food to the meetings on the children's behalf, as their offerings to the Devil.) Finally, the Devil would strip the new witches and wizards of their clothing, and the whole company would reaffirm their allegiance by filing past the Devil to kiss his buttocks.

Then the music and dancing would begin. The Devil played the flute, and demons and witches, dancing back to back, would wildly circle round him, stamping, singing and capering with indecent gestures. Or sometimes the unbridled dance took the form of "follow-my-leader", the Devil leading them wherever he would. Eventually, the festivities developed into a sexual orgy which lasted until the break of dawn. Incest ran rife, and the witches all coupled with demons, for the Devil became an incubus to women and a succubus to men. (It was explained that the Devil seduced male and female witches because both were addicted to carnal pleasures, and he "bound them to his allegiance by such agreeable provocations". During witch-trials, the women all denied finding intercourse with the Devil pleasurable. In the form of a black man, cat, dog, ram or goat, they found him repulsive; penetration was accompanied by pain as great as that of childbirth, and they all agreed that his penis and semen were as cold as ice. Nevertheless, the Devil claimed that "there is nothing which makes a woman more subject and loyal to a man than that he should abuse her body", and he never ran out of semen since his supply was replenished when he took the form of a succubus.)

It is said that, during the reign of Charles IX, there were 30,000 sorcerers and witches in Paris, and 100,000 scattered throughout the rest of France. Sabbats were celebrated from the fifteenth to the end of the eighteenth centuries, and many

18. Pompeian cat pouncing on a bird *p. 73*

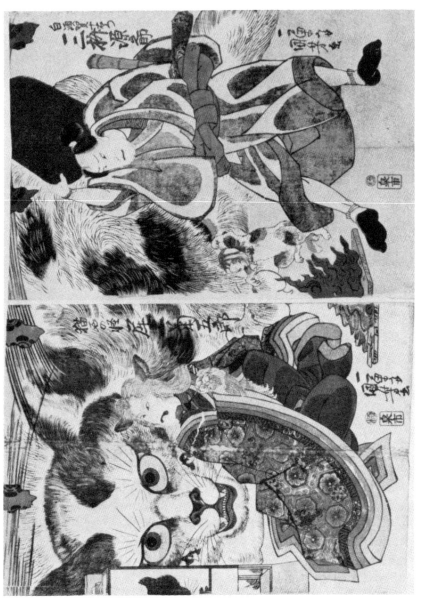

19. Okabe witch being transformed into a cat *p. 84*

wealthy and aristocratic people gathered to watch these throngs performing their rites.

The black cat had, however, been worshipped as an incarnation of the Devil several centuries before the Sabbats became established. For, whereas the Devil was first revealed to women in the form of a toad or a goose and not until much later as a cat, he appeared in feline form to male heretics as early as the thirteenth century. (Heretics have indeed been likened to cats. A seventeenth-century friar gave the warning to the faithful that "the heretic can creep secretly where no man seeth him as doth also the cat who can make herself soft and secret. . . ". He went on to explain that cats lick poisonous toads and then drink water which is drawn on by humans; consequently, ". . . the cat will defile the body, the heretic defileth the soul".) In accounts of nocturnal rites which were alleged to have been practised by members of mediaeval secret societies, many references are to be found to the part played by a black tom-cat.

One of the most famous of such secret societies was that of the Knights Templars. At the beginning of the twelfth century, nine French knights united and dedicated themselves to the protection of Christians who were making pilgrimages to the Holy Land and were being persecuted by Moslems. They became known as the Templars, because their arms were kept in a building on the site of the old Temple of Solomon at Jerusalem. The numbers of these brethren rapidly increased; and, when they received the sanction of the Church, they took the three vows of poverty, chastity and obedience common to all religious orders. Their reputation was very high indeed, and they were loved and respected by all who came in contact with them. They took a prominent part in the Crusades, and over the next two hundred years the influence of the Knights Templars spread throughout the whole of Europe.

But subsequently something went wrong within this Order, for, in spite of its members' vows, it grew immensely rich and powerful, and gradually became corrupt. The respect which the Templars had aroused was replaced in all strata of society by antagonism. The nobility regarded them with envy and fear, the clergy had many grievances against them, and the lower classes resented their tyranny and arrogance. The beginning of the fourteenth century brought their final downfall when they were confronted with open accusations, by the pope and Philip IV of France, of heresy, treachery and immorality. All French members of the Order were immediately arrested and imprisoned, and many of them were tried and burnt at the stake.

Rumours had been circulating for some years that, although the Templars professed Christianity, the secret midnight meetings they held were often scenes of idolatry and blasphemous rites, and their rule of chastity had been used as a cover for homosexual orgies. During the trials of the Knights Templars, confessions were extracted under torture of ceremonies that were very similar to those practised by witches at their Sabbats. They were accused of, and admitted to, trampling or spitting on the Cross, and worshipping the Devil in the form of a black tom-cat. It was described how the cat, which appeared among the participants, stood by an idol and was ritually kissed by them all under its tail. No one seemed to know where the animal came from or where it went when they adjourned, but it was generally assumed to have embodied the Devil.

The Templars were not by any means the only sect accused of worshipping a black cat. Manicheans, the disciples of Mani, the Persian prophet, believed that the human race was of Satanic origin and that the powers of darkness were as strong as the powers of light. They felt it necessary to be continually placating the Devil, who seems to have had a predilection for feline form. (Cats glutted with prey are occasionally to be found depicted in churches on pillars and pulpits. And some antiquarians maintain that these were carved by mediaeval stone-masons who were tainted with the Manichean heresy.)

Members of this sect would scuttle through dark streets, carrying lanterns, to the house where their secret meetings were held. On arrival, they would chant the names of various demons as an evocative liturgy, until suddenly the Devil would himself appear in their midst in the form of a black tom-cat. This was the signal for all lights to be extinguished, and for members to seize the women nearest them. When, as the result of these orgies, a child was born, an assembly would be called eight days after its birth at which a large fire would be lit and the infant ceremonially passed through the flames. Its ashes were collected and preserved, for it was claimed that anyone who tasted them would never abandon his heresies. It was also said that the ritual violation of a virgin had its place among Manichean rites.

The Luciferans were another similar heretical sect. They believed that the Devil had been driven out of heaven unjustly, and would one day be restored to his former glory. They were reputed to worship a black cat at their midnight assemblies, to sacrifice young children, and to use their blood for making eucharistic bread.

An eleventh-century reform movement, the Waldensians, made themselves obnoxious to the ecclesiastical powers and met with terrible persecution. Members of this society confessed that the Devil appeared to them as a cat, and was ritually kissed *sub cauda* by the celebrants. When being attacked by royal troops, the Waldensians are said to have summoned the Devil to their aid, and it was this that repeatedly enabled them to escape. The Paturini, a contemporary sect of the Waldensians, described how they sang hymns until dusk, when a black tom-cat would be lowered among them. At this moment the lights were put out, and devotion would soon give way to sexual licence. At the orgies of a thirteenth-century German sect known as the Stedingers, a statue of a large black cat was exhibited.

Since the Devil was expected to manifest himself as an animal, the cat was certainly an appropriate form for him to choose. For not only is the tom an exceedingly lustful creature, which will become impervious even to hunger in the vicinity of a female on heat, but it is easy to imagine that the glint of its eyes in the darkness and the sparks which its fur emits on a frosty night could, given a sympathetic atmosphere, readily produce a sense of demonic power. The cat is considered by many occultists to be a highly magnetized animal, and it is on just such forces that magicians draw, exploiting them for personal gain.

Most of the confessions of these dark practices involving cats were obtained, as in the case of witch-trials, as a result of racking and every other kind of torture. Whether the rites attributed to these particular mediaeval societies were in detail true or false will probably never be ascertained. But the many rumours, accusations and confessions do at least point to a popular *belief* that such things existed during these centuries.

The Demon

When the black cat appeared as an embodiment of the Devil, all known aspects of evil were presumably focused in it. But sometimes the powers of darkness were split up, and the cat would appear in a variety of demonic guises.

In some of the earliest legends, feline demons emerged from water. An ancient Chinese work tells of a cat which was owned by an emperor. It was bathing in a pool of water after three days of rain, when it was suddenly transformed into a dragon and flew off, never to be seen again.

As a beast of prey, the cat is a monster of fur, fangs and claws. Its greatest force lies in its claws, and when these seize its prey their grip is so tenacious that nothing can break it. (It is significant that the Devil has been known as "Old Scratch", a Scandinavian equivalent of "Old Nick".)

One of the world's greatest stories of heroic combat must surely be that in which the legendary King Arthur fought in Switzerland with a monstrous cat. A fourteenth-century French manuscript, *Le Roman de Merlin*, gives a lively if blood-curdling account of this fight, which was among Arthur's most dangerous exploits.

It first tells of a man who was fishing one day in Lake Geneva, and caught in his net a black kitten. He fed it and gave it a home, but it soon grew much larger than most cats, and finally it strangled not only the befriending fisherman but also his wife and children. After this, the monster fled to the mountains – "a catte, full of the devell that is so grete and ougly, that it is a horrible sight on to loke" – and it became the terror of the countryside, destroying all who came within its reach.

So Arthur and his knights, led by the magician, Merlin, set out to encounter this feline demon. After they had climbed up a mountainside, Merlin pointed out the deep cave which he knew to be the cat's lair, and he warned the heroes to be ready to defend themselves. When they had all drawn back, he whistled to rouse the animal. Immediately, it appeared at the entrance and took one great leap at Arthur. The king received this onslaught with his spear, but the cat broke the weapon to pieces in its mouth. Then the ferocious beast sprang at Arthur's throat, but he used his shield so expertly that it fell to the ground. After Arthur had struck the cat on its head so that the skin was cut by his sword, the animal seized him by the shoulders and its claws penetrated his armour, drawing blood. An enraged Arthur again attacked the cat, but it rushed at him and fixed its claws in his shield so that they could not be extricated. The king had to cut its forelegs off; but, when he ran with his sword towards the fallen cat, it flew at his throat, gripping him with its hind feet, and biting his chest and shoulders till they were streaming with blood.

Arthur finally managed to free himself, but only by cutting off its hind legs. The mutilated monster again fell to the ground, and began to slither off in the direction of its cave. Then, the heroic struggle at an end, Arthur pressed forward and killed the cat.

From then on the mountain called "du lac" was known as "du chat". It was said that Arthur disappeared after this terrible fight, and there is a tradition that he was actually slain by the cat.

An early Welsh legend tells of a savage kitten with which Arthur was indirectly connected, and which grew up to be one of the Three Plagues of Anglesey. In about 800 B.C., the Britons worshipped Cerridwen, the Mother Goddess, who often took the form of a sow. The legend tells how a sow called Henwen, who was very big with young, lived in Cornwall where she was tended by her keeper, Coll. It had been prophesied that Britain would be injured by her progeny, so, when Henwen was about to farrow, Arthur collected together the country's forces and set out to destroy her. He chased her down to Land's End but did not kill her, for she swam out to sea with the swineherd hanging on to her by her bristles.

The huge sow landed at a number of places, and in them she brought forth three grains of wheat, one of barley, one grain of rye, three bees, a pig, a wolf-cub and an eaglet – for all of which gifts the places became famous. Finally, Henwen landed with Coll at Arvon, and here, under a black stone, she bore a kitten. The swineherd threw the kitten into the Menai Straits, but the sons of Paluc, from the Isle of Man, rescued and reared it. By so doing they brought disaster to their country, for it was this kitten which became the ferocious Paluc cat which was notorious as the molester of the Isle of Man.

(Wild cats are, of course, notoriously fierce and will attack a man without provocation. The cat-a-mountain haunts heraldic devices, and the Mackintosh family's motto: "Touch not a cat but [without] a glove", is an indication of this animal's reputation. It is significant that the French name for a wild cat is *haret*, a word cognate with the English "harry", which is associated with pillage, plunder and destruction.)

In a legend concerning St Brendan, a Celtic saint, reference is made to a great sea-cat. When St Brendan arrived at an unknown island, he made his way to the church, where he found an old man. The old man warned him: "O holy man of God, make haste to flee from this island. For there is a sea-cat here, of old time, inveterate in wiles, that hath grown huge through eating excessively of fish". The saint and his disciples caught a glimpse of the feline monster swimming through the sea, and described it as having great eyes "like vessels of glass".

The Celts believed cats to be supernatural, "druidic" beasts, and Celtic heroes often had stinging cats to contend with. Cuchulainn, and two other heroes of Irish saga, were attacked in a cave one night by three magic cats, which disappeared at the break of dawn. When one of the cats stretched its neck out for food, Cuchulainn gave its head a blow with his sword, but the blade slid off it as if from stone. In Irish folk-tales demons were often described as ferocious black cats with blazing eyes. Typical is the story of one which terrified a woman by leaping through a window into her living-room. Luckily a priest had just come in through the door and, after he had sprinkled the demon with holy water, it subsided and its eyes appeared as glowing coals on the hearth.

From the East come stories of phantom-cats; and the Japanese (to whom the cat is a "tiger who eats from the hand") have a legend which tells of a feline jinn which annually demanded human sacrifice. A knight, who was travelling in the mountains, spent the night in a ruined temple. Just before midnight, he was abruptly awakened and found beside him a number of ghostly cats, which were dancing and loudly chanting: "Don't tell Shippeitaro about it." When midnight struck, however, they disappeared. Next day, when the knight resumed his travels, he came to a village whose inhabitants appeared to be very distressed. They explained to him that the day had arrived on which the annual tribute must be paid to the feline jinn of the mountain. The most beautiful maiden of the village had to be put in a cage; the terrible phantom-cat would drag her to its lair (the ruined temple) and there it would slowly devour her.

On hearing this pathetic tale, the knight, recalling his experience of the previous evening, asked who Shippeitaro was. He was told that it was the name of a big brave dog which belonged to the local prince. "Ah," thought the knight, "he surely could disperse those phantom-cats." So he went to the prince and, having explained the plight of the villagers to him, soon returned with Shippeitaro and put him in the cage prepared for the victim. Helped by village youths, the knight then carried the litter to the temple, where he and

Shippeitaro kept watch until midnight. When the phantom-cats appeared, they had with them as their leader an enormous tom-cat, which prowled round the cage uttering screams of anticipatory delight. Suddenly the knight flung open the cage-door and Shippeitaro sprang forth, grabbing the great monster between his teeth. In a flash the knight had drawn his sword and succeeded in slaying the ferocious beast. Shippeitaro soon dispersed the rest of the cats, and the village was released from its annual persecution. Plate 22 is an illustration of a Japanese hero killing such a monster-cat.

In the sixth century, the Chinese believed in cat-spectres. An ancient story is told of a man called T'o, whose mother was said to serve a cat-spectre. When cat-spectres killed anybody, the possessions of the victim were secretly drawn to the house which the demon frequented. In A.D. 595, according to the story, the empress was suffering from an unaccountable illness. People said that T'o, who wanted money for liquor, had persuaded his mother to utter her spells and send the cat-spectre to the palace to bewitch the empress into bestowing gifts on him.

The emperor was advised that the only way to put an end to spectral evil was by killing the person from whom it emanated. So, the next time T'o's female slave appeared at the palace gate, she was met by police and told to call back the cat-spectre. This she did by setting out a bowl of rice-gruel and drumming on it with a spoon. When the cat-spectre answered her call, the slave went blue in the face and moved about as if she were being trailed. The emperor was on the point of ordering T'o and his wife to commit suicide, when T'o's brother arrived at the palace and, on their behalf, begged for mercy. So T'o was granted his life, but he was divested of all his dignities and his wife was made a Buddhist nun. The emperor lost no time in seeking out all families who kept cat-spectres, and he banished them to remote parts of China.

It was believed by the Chinese of this period that, after death, people sometimes changed themselves into cats in order to take revenge on their enemies. A court lady, whose empress had sentenced her to death, threatened to return and change the latter into a rat so that, in cat-form, she could throttle her. (Orientals say that if you are afraid of cats you must have been a rat in your last incarnation.)

There are European tales of cat-goblins. In some parts of Provence, for instance, people say that it is unwise for travellers to answer anyone who speaks to them after sundown. The danger is that they might be accosted by one of those earth spirits which are neither good enough to be angels nor bad enough to be devils, but are mischievous to human beings. Such demons most often appear as cats, with blazing eyes and pale luminous bodies. They move with supernatural speed, so it is useless to try to run away from them. The only advice given to travellers who meet cat-goblins is to cover their eyes, call on their saints for help, and make for the nearest lighted cottage. Slavic peasants try to avoid meeting black cats late at night, for they believe them to be demonic, and liable to seize and destroy lonely travellers.

Stories are told in the Scottish Highlands of elfin cats, described as large black beasts, with arched backs, erect bristles, and white spots dotted over their chests. Cats of the Isle of Man are said to have their own king. This king, we are told, appears as an ordinary cat during the day, but at night, when he assumes full regal powers, he travels across the countryside in a fiery state (recalling the cat of the Celtic myth of Maeldune). If anyone has treated him badly during the daytime, he will seek him out and take terrible vengeance on him.

As we all know cats are natural tormentors, and the cruel way in which they play with their wounded prey has become proverbial. To "play cat and mouse" is to pretend to let go someone in your power while in fact you are still holding him a prisoner. People who lived within the sphere of action of any of these feline demons must have known what it was like "to live under the cat's paw", for they appear to have enjoyed an untormented existence only on the cat's sufferance.

The Vampire

We come now to the type of cat-phantom which preys on the lives of human beings in what is perhaps the most pernicious way of all.

The succubus and incubus are lascivious female and male spirits which have sexual intercourse with men and women at night, draining off their natural vitality. We have already seen how, at the Sabbats, the Devil, often in feline form, would split himself up into succubi and incubi in order to couple with the sorcerers and witches. A seventeenth-century document records the confession made by a Suffolk witch that ". . . the Devil did appear in the form of a Pretty hansom Young Man first, and since Appeareth to her in the form of a blackish Gray Cat or Kitling, and that it sucketh of a Tett."

The arch drainer-of-life is the vampire, and it is specifically a sucker of men's blood. We have already seen how cat-familiars sucked the blood of the witches they served, but this was a different phenomenon, since the witch voluntarily entered into this relationship with the cat, encouraging it to drink her blood, which she offered as a reward for services rendered. No one has ever encouraged the act of a vampire; it always sucks the blood of the living in violation of their will.

Vampires have often taken feline form. A Japanese legend called "The Cat of Nabéshima" tells the story of an erotic cat-vampire. The Prince of Hizen, a member of the honoured Nabéshima family, had as his favourite concubine a charming woman whose name was O Toyo. One evening, the lovers wandered into the garden and stayed out enjoying the flowers until sunset. When eventually they were returning to the palace, they did not realize that a cat was following them.

O Toyo retired to her own room and went to sleep. But at midnight, awaking with a start, she became aware of being watched by a huge double-tailed crouching cat. Before she could cry out for help, it sprang at her throat and throttled her to death. The cat then scratched a hole under the verandah, buried O Toyo, and assumed her form. The prince knew nothing of this tragedy, and had no idea that the beautiful woman who came and made love to him every night was in fact a demon who was draining his life's blood. Day by day the Prince of Hizen's strength dwindled; his face became pale and livid, and he appeared to be suffering from fatal illness. He took all the medicines prescribed for him by doctors but none of them did him any good.

Since his sufferings always increased at night, it was arranged that a hundred servants should form a guard every evening when he went to bed. The watchers took up their positions, but just before ten o'clock they were overcome by drowsiness, and the vampire preyed on her victim as usual. Each night events followed the same course and the prince's health grew steadily worse. His councillors began to realize that they were up against something supernatural, and they turned for help to the chief priest of the temple, begging him to pray for the prince's recovery. The prayers of the priest were disturbed by a noise in the garden, and he discovered there a soldier called Ito Soda, who served in the infantry of Nabéshima. This young man begged to be allowed to sit up one night with the prince, to try to resist the drowsiness and detect the evil spirit.

His request was eventually granted, and when, at ten o'clock, he felt the drowsiness beginning to steal over him, he thrust his dagger into his thigh so that the sharp pain would keep him awake. He watched the sliding doors of the prince's room open, and in stole a beautiful young woman who made her way to the bedside. Suddenly, however, she became aware that there was present someone who was still awake, and she spoke to him, asking who he was. Several times she approached the sick prince to cast her spells on him, but, so long as Ito Soda was glaring at her, she was powerless and had to retire, leaving the prince undisturbed. On the following night, the same thing happened again, and as a result of the soldier's vigilance the vampire returned frustrated to her apartments. When the prince had had two undisturbed nights, his health began to improve. The vampire, after several more fruitless visits, kept away, and the night guards ceased to be overcome by drowsiness.

It had now become obvious to Ito that the being who appeared at nights as O Toyo was really a ghoul, and he made plans to kill her forthwith. At nightfall, the soldier went to her apartment, pretending that he had a message for her from the prince. As he approached he struck at her with his dagger, but she sprang away and picked up a halberd. Finding, however, that she was no match for Ito Soda, the woman transformed herself into a cat and, springing on to the roof, she managed to escape to the mountains. The cat-demon harried local inhabitants until one day the prince, having fully regained his health, was able to organize a great hunt. He succeeded in avenging his beautiful concubine, for the vampire-cat of Nabéshima was finally destroyed.

(The *Sunday Express* of 14th July, 1929, published the following report from Japan: "The vampire-cat of Nabéshima is once more about its nightly business, bewitching the beautiful wives of the descendants of the old two-sworded fighting Samurai.") Plate 23 is an illustration of the vampire's attack on the beautiful O Toyo.

According to Hebrew folklore, Adam had a wife before Eve was formed, and her name was Lilith. Lilith, however, refused to submit to Adam, so she departed from Paradise and ever since has haunted the night. Spanish Jews believe that Lilith became a vampire, and that her favourite victims are infants. It is in the form of a huge black cat called El Broosha that Lilith is said to suck the blood of new-born babes.

Although these are all examples of vampirism where the word is used in its broader sense, strictly speaking a vampire is the revived body of a dead person which sucks the blood of the living during their sleep. Sometimes the vampire is a blood-sucking ghost, and when its victims are heretics or criminals they usually themselves become vampires.

In some parts of eastern Europe, however, there was a belief that even an innocent man may become a vampire if a cat crosses his corpse before its burial, for the cat is thought to be a potential vampire which can infect the corpse by its mere proximity. In Northumbria, cats that accidentally walk or leap across a corpse will, for the same reason, often be put to death.

A seventeenth-century account of vampirism describes the case of a Silesian, called Johannes Cuntius, who died at the age of sixty as the result of a kick from his horse. At the moment of his death a black cat rushed into his room, jumped onto the bed and scratched violently at his face. After the funeral, stories of the appearance of a phantom, which spoke to people in the voice of Cuntius, began to circulate. Tales were told of the disappearance of milk from jugs and bowls, of milk being turned into blood, of altar-cloths being soiled with blood, of old men being strangled, of children stolen from cradles, and of poultry being killed and eaten.

After six months of such incidents it was decided to disinter Cuntius's body. It was found that, whereas all the bodies laid above that of Cuntius were putrefied, his skin had remained tender and florid, his joints were still flexible, and when a staff was placed between his fingers they firmly grasped it. He could open and close his eyes, and, when a vein in his leg was punctured, the blood sprang out as fresh as that of a living person. The authorities knew that they must dismember and cremate the body of Johannes Cuntius. They had great difficulty in cutting up the limbs, for they offered considerable resistance, but, once the task was completed and the remains had been burnt, the spectre was never seen again.

In times past, when someone in China died, the family showed great anxiety to transfer all the house-cats to neighbours, or, alternatively, they would tie them up until the body was in its coffin. The danger they spoke of was that any cat might possess a "soul-recalling hair", and, if it did and walked or leapt over a death-bed, the corpse was liable to rise up. The only remedy for such a disaster was to take a pole, a broomhandle or a piece of furniture, and offer it to the corpse. The latter, who would probably be frantic with rage, would grasp the pole with both hands, pulling it against its chest to cool its wrath, and with any luck would sink back into an inert state. If a relative allowed himself to be seized instead of a broom, a horrible death awaited him in the corpse's ferocious embrace.

The "soul-recalling hair" was really the property of tigers. The Chinese believed that the tiger had a miraculous hair in its tail which had the power of bringing back the soul to a dead body. It was said that, when a tiger dragged a man into a mountain cave, it would wave its tail around and over him. This was to ensure that his soul would return after death so that he had to undergo a second agony. During the second death-pangs, he was likely to tear off all his clothes, thus sparing the tiger any obstruction to its meal.

Every hour, day, month and year of the Chinese calendar came under the special influence of animals, one of which was the tiger. So, apart from the fact that the cat might, on account of its close resemblance to the tiger, happen to possess a "soul recalling hair" which would cause the dead person to become a vampire, there was a special risk involved on "tiger-days", when the feline influence was predominant.

The Bewitcher

If you watch a cat with its prey, there are moments when you feel the victim could still escape, but it appears to be paralysed or apathetic. It is as if cats, like snakes, almost cast a spell on their prey.

Cats are generally unpopular in Japan, because they are believed to have the power to bewitch people. The word "cat" is sometimes applied to a geisha. The grace and beauty of a cat's lithe and sinuous body are associated with that of the "singing girl", who has the power of bewitching the opposite sex. The geisha's victim has been represented as a "cat-fish", for he allows himself to be captured and subjugated by a beautiful and fascinating creature.

There is a Buddhist fable which attempts to illustrate the

20. Witches with cat-familiars preparing for the Sabbat *p. 90*

66.

Ensayos.

21. Witch with devil-cats teaching a sorcerer to levitate *p. 92*

belief that women resemble cats in that they seek to ruin anyone who comes within their power. The Buddha had taken
the form of a cockerel living among many other cocks. A she-
cat, who had succeeded in hoodwinking all the other birds so
that she could eat them, finally turned her wiles towards the
cock which incarnated the Buddha. But, although she offered
him perpetual youth and beauty, and the choice of a simple
slave-girl or an honoured wife, he withstood her attractions
and eventually drove her away: "For," said the enlightened
cockerel, "there is no honour in your heart when you are
wooing me."

The power of the legendary cat to bewitch seems to have
been focused in its tail. It was claimed that forked- or double-
tailed Japanese cat-demons, such as that shown in Plate 23,
had doubly strong powers of bewitchment. The Irish had
two-tailed and ten-tailed magical cats. (The cat-o'-nine-tails
was, of course, an emblem of power, although in this case the
power was that of royalty.) The Japanese maintained that,
although cats had a natural tendency to become demons, this
could be checked by cutting off their tails while they were still
kittens.

In Mme D'Aulnoy's "The White Cat", it was not until the
tail of the white cat had been cut off and flung into the fire that
the princess and her entire court were released from the
bewitchment which they had suffered for so long. Plate 24
illustrates this operation.

A famous story of the severed tail of a cat (though in this
case there is no mention of bewitchment) is one which
accounts for the taillessness of the Manx. The oldest version of
this legend describes how the cat was the last of all animals to
enter the Ark, for it would not go in without taking a
mouse with it. When Noah had all the other animals safely
inside and the rain was beginning to fall, there was still no

sign of the cat. Eventually, however, she turned up and was squeezing through the door as Noah slammed it. So, since the tail of the half-drowned cat was cut off, she went into the Ark without it. Another version describes how:

> Noah, sailing o'er the seas
> Ran fast aground on Ararat;
> His dog then made a spring and took
> The tail from off a pretty cat.
> Puss through the window quick did fly,
> And bravely through the waters swam
> Nor ever stopped till high and dry,
> She landed on the Calf of Man.
> Thus tailless Puss earned Mona's thanks
> And ever after was called Manx.

The Traitor

There is a dark aspect of the cat's reputation which is not based on belief in its supernatural power, but has arisen more directly from its observed natural behaviour.

Cats are notorious for their fickleness and unpredictability, an added reason, perhaps, for associating them with geishas! Egyptians punished faithless women for their adultery by tying them up in a sack with a cat, and flinging the sack into the Nile. The same fate befell inconstant Icelandic wives, the sacks being flung into a "Drowning Pool".

The nature of the cat's eyes aptly expresses this aspect of its character. The semi-precious stone known as "cat's eye" is so called because it possesses chatoyancy, that is a change-ability in lustre and colour like the eyes of a cat in the dark.

To "turn cat-in-pan" means to be a traitor or a turncoat. As Bacon explains in his essay "Of cunning": "There is a cunning which we in England call the turning of a cat in the pan which is, when that which a man says to another, he lays it as if another had said it to him." It may be true, as the dictionary claims, that the phrase derives from the French *tourner côte en peine* (to turn sides in trouble), but the fact that we have chosen this corruption, and that it has stuck, is probably because it is also true about cats!

The cat that, at the time of the first French Republic, was a symbol of liberty, later came to represent perfidy. The frontispiece of an old volume entitled *Les crimes des papes* showed a cat at the feet of the pope, where it symbolized treason and hypocrisy.

It was traditional in Italian art to introduce a cat into paintings of the Last Supper, and this animal has appeared too often at the feet of the traitor, Judas Iscariot, for its location not to be significant. Plate 25 shows a portion of Luini's "Last Supper": here we find Judas clutching his bag of silver, with a striped cat curling its tail between his feet. A fresco by Ghirlandajo shows Judas sitting apart from the other apostles with only a cat to keep him company, and one of Cellini's bas-reliefs shows a cat at the feet of Judas.

The Trickster

The means employed by natural cats to secure their prey have always been ingenious, and there are many fables in which the cat set out deliberately to trick, and to take advantage of, more gullible animals. It is portrayed as a gifted actor, a first class strategist and a great fraud. La Fontaine shows the cat as being even more cunning than the fox, for, although both are hypocrites and swindlers, in the last resort the cunning tricks of the cat prove superior to those of the fox.

The "Penitent Cat" has become proverbial, and a typical story is to be found in the Indian epic, the Mahabharata. There was a cat who sat on the banks of the River Ganges, feigning penitence for all his sins, particularly those of cruelty to other animals. For days he practised austerities by the river, gradually building up a reputation for saintliness. The asceticism of this holy animal inspired confidence in the birds and mice of the whole area, and they gathered around him in great numbers, to do him honour and to put themselves under his protection. Every day, when the cat was surrounded by trustful prey, he would lead them to the river, presumably to wash away their sins. And it was always during this "mystical" experience that the cat had his main meal of the day!

Another cat who had repented of all his crimes was called upon to act as judge in a dispute which had arisen between a sparrow and a hare. Unfortunately, the judge appeared to have become stone-deaf, and he begged the sparrow and the hare to come near to him and confide their arguments in his ear. With complete faith in the cat's reformation, they approached him and were both promptly devoured.

Aesop tells of a cat who made no pretence of repentance, but rather fancied himself as an actor. He happened to hear that there was sickness among the birds in a nearby aviary, so he dressed himself up to look like a physician and set out, complete with a cane and bag of instruments. Presenting himself at the aviary, he inquired after the health of the sick birds and offered to prescribe remedies for all their ills. On this occasion, however, his ingenuity failed, for the birds smelt not a rat but a cat!

Egyptian fables tell of cats who force their services on animals which they intend later to devour, and there is a papyrus which shows a cat, dressed as a peasant, driving a flock of geese with a stick.

An Italian fable describes the adventures of a cock who wanted to be pope. The foolish bird accepted the offer, made by his friend, the cat, to accompany him to Rome, and was eaten on the first day's journey. La Fontaine describes the antics of a cat called Rodilard, who was the scourge and terror of all the mice and rats. One day, Rodilard was feeling peckish, so he devised a means of procuring a real feast. He hung himself upside down beside a wall – "... resisting gravitation's laws ..." – but, although he appeared to have been hanged, in fact he held a hidden cord in his claws. The mice, believing that Rodilard had at last received his due for all the crimes he had mercilessly committed, thronged round him in the highest of spirits, and then ran off to spread the glad news to the rats. Rats and mice in their dozens soon appeared and wandered blissfully around hunting for food, exploiting to the full their false security. Their joy was, however, short-lived, for suddenly Rodilard pulled at the cord, sprang to the floor and was soon gorging himself on the victims of his stratagem (Plate 26).

But even this was not the end of his tricks, for it annoyed Rodilard that a number of mice had escaped into their holes. So he found some meal and covered the whole of his body with it, then:

> Squatted in an open tub
> And held his purring and his breath,
> Till out came the vermin to their death.

A relief in a Spanish cathedral shows a stately pageant entitled "Execution of the Cat". This piece of sculpture illustrates the story of a tabby which is at the usual trick of pretending to be dead. It lies on a bier, borne by a long procession of rodents carrying banners, vessels of holy water, aspergills, crosiers and censers. The executioner, a rat with an axe, marches with official dignity under the litter. A second scene shows the cat pouncing on the rat, while the other members of the cortège disperse in all directions, scattering the paraphernalia over the ground.

The saying "to let the cat out of the bag" means to give away a secret, and it is closely linked with "a pig in a poke". Country people would bring a bag to market which they said contained a sucking pig but for which they had in fact substituted a cat. If the purchaser was gullible enough to buy "a pig in a poke" without examination, the owner got away with it; but if the buyer opened the carrier, then he "let the cat out of the bag".

There is an interesting German version of this. The phrase *die Katze im Sack kaufen* is connected with obtaining a "broody" coin (one which will produce many more), and the imaginary pig is replaced by an imaginary hare. A man would put a black cat into a bag on the longest night of the year. He tied the string of the bag with ninety-nine knots, and carried the bag three times round the church, calling out to the sacristan that he had a hare for sale. Eventually, the sacristan would appear and give the man a broody coin in exchange for the bag. The man then raced home as fast as his legs would carry him, for if he failed to get there before the knots were untied and the sacristan had "let the cat out of the bag", he would surely be hounded by bad luck. So, in both cases, we find the notorious trickster himself being used in a trick.

In addition to its penchant for trickery, the cat, with its padded feet and stealthy approach, is undeniably a thief (or "pussyfoot"). In fact, the same word appears to have been used in Sanskrit for both cats and thieves! Not only does the cat steal fish and meat intended for human consumption, but it will deprive other animals of hard-won meals. So associated is the cat with theft that Hungarian peasants insist that only a stolen cat will make a good mouser. This particular character-trait resulted in cats' becoming the victims of an odious rite practised in southern Slavonia. Here a thief would blind a cat and then burn it, for he believed that, if he threw a pinch of its ashes over the man he intended to burgle, he had every chance of getting away with his crime.

Both the cat's habitual thieving and many of its tricks described in the fables arise out of, and serve, its innate laziness. There is a story of a cat and sparrows, in which the cat pretends to allow the hungry birds to eat bread and then eats them. And there is another about a cat-and-mouse partnership, in which the cat tricks the mouse into obtaining food, and then eats the mouse. The cat will let its head rule its heart in order to indulge its love of comfort and get food without the effort of hunting for it. The old adage, "All cats love fish but fear to wet their paws", refers to someone who, like the cat, is anxious to possess something valuable, but is unwilling to take the trouble or risk necessary to acquire it.

In Christian symbolism the cat sometimes represents apathy. The "copy-cat" is someone who slavishly imitates another, instead of relying on his own inspiration. (This has probably arisen from the cat's imitative ability, for kittens are taught to copy the habits of one another, and in some cases even of human beings.)

Although cats appear to have perfectly good memories, they are associated in folklore with forgetfulness, which again points to a certain sluggishness. In Russia, Jewish boys were not allowed to stroke a cat lest they lose their memories. This may possibly have been due to the fact that cats eat mice, and mice are considered to be a cause of forgetfulness. It is said that the kink in the tail of a Siamese cat is to remind it of something which it has not yet remembered!

The gib-cat is renowned for its melancholy, another state of lowered vitality. A naturalist writing in 1843 said, "Most of the former [he-cats] that are kept are emasculated, in which state, always accompanied with a subdued and melancholy appearance, they are called Gilberts or Gib-cats." A joke has to be very funny indeed if it is to be "enough to make a cat laugh". And the false grin of the "Cheshire Cat" presumably covers a sinking heart.

If these traits are sins, they are sins of omission; but somehow this inability to "come up to scratch" seems to underlie many of the cat's more active crimes.

The Fighter

The fighting instinct is exceptionally strong in cats, the males beginning to fight as soon as they reach maturity. Often their fights last many hours, for much time is spent glaring at, and stalking, each other with backs arched and hackles risen. From time to time, blood-curdling screams rise from their choking throats.

There is an ancient story of a Persian king called Hormus, who found himself besieged by rebels. A wise old man appeared and told the king that he could rout the enemy in a single day if he was able to find a cat-faced man to lead his officers. Eventually, a cat-faced mountaineer was found and the king immediately made him a general. Such was his prowess that, with only twelve thousand men at his disposal, he beat an enemy army of three hundred thousand.

Tales are told of cat-headed Irish warriors. Like the Irish king known as "Carbar of the Cat's Head", they wore

helmets entirely covered with skins of wild cats, which gave
the impression of their being cat-headed.

Battles between cats and rats (like the one in "The White
Cat") have been popular literary subjects. Although the cat
is a terrific fighter, it is not, however, always depicted as the
winner.

An Egyptian papyrus depicts a great battle between armies
of cats and rats in which the rats seem to be getting the best
of it. (It is virtually a parody of battle-scenes of the nineteenth
dynasty pharaohs which decorate walls of Theban temples.)
The rat-pharaoh stands upright in a chariot drawn by dogs,
and is leading his army against cats who are defending a
fort. The rats, gracefully poised with bows, shower the enemy
with arrows and their steeds trample on the fallen cats.

A famous Persian story, written by a fourteenth-century
satirist, tells of a battle of "Rats against Cats". The army
of cats was led by ". . . a dragon of a cat, drum-bellied, shield-
chested, serpent-tailed, eagle-clawed", and the rats were led
by an astute, brave and judicious rat, commanding three
hundred and thirty thousand soldiers armed with bows and
arrows, lances and swords. The two mounted armies met in
an open plain and fought bravely with huge casualties. The
cats finally charged at the heart of the rats' army, spreading
confusion in their ranks. But just when the rats appeared to
have lost the battle, one of them felled the horse of the cats'
leader. Quickly the cat was bound and taken to the rat-king,
and the rats beat drums of joy as the leaderless cat-army broke
up and dispersed in shame.

"To fight like Kilkenny cats" means to fight, with determination and pertinacity, until both sides have lost everything. The saying derives from the story that, during the
Irish rebellion, Kilkenny was garrisoned by a troop of
soldiers who amused themselves by tying two cats together

by their tails and throwing them across a clothes-line to fight. When the officer on duty appeared, one of the soldiers cut the two tails with a sword and the cats made off. When the officer asked about the bleeding tails, he was told that two cats had been fighting and had devoured each other except for the tails. This story is a most distasteful one, but is typical of the kind of thing cats attract to themselves.

There is a German belief that, to an invalid, the sight of two cats fighting is an omen of approaching death. Tuscan children play a game, known as the "game of souls"; and it has been suggested that the two German cats play the same role as the Devil and angel who come to dispute for the soul in the Tuscan game.

Petty malice – a spitting sort of spite that goes by the name of "cattiness" – is very liable to lead to squabbling. Aesop has expressed the intense aversion that naturally exists between cats and dogs, describing a pair who were:

> . . . Often falling into strife
> Which came to scratching, growls and snaps,
> And spitting in the face, perhaps.

People who are always quarrelling, like the animals in Plate 27, are said to lead a "cat-and-dog life".

The Victim

Eventually, the "blackness" of the cat caught up with it, and Plate 28, showing a cat captured and tormented by rats, is a Japanese interpretation of a scene of final retribution. There is a popular Russian print which shows a triumphant procession of forty-four mice dragging a bound cat on a sledge.

Such situations were very popular among satirists. Misericords of rats hanging a cat are to be found in the Priory Church of Great Malvern and in Worcester Cathedral; and, as we have already seen, battles staged between rats and cats often show the rats getting their own back.

The cat, however, received its consistent and most terrible persecution not from rats but at the hands of human beings.

Cats have been sacrificed for diverse reasons. No doubt the experience was always much the same for the cats, but to those who perpetrated the deed it often felt quite different, and it is important to distinguish between the various human motives involved. We have already seen how, because of the "lightness" of feline nature, the cat was once regarded as a god and as such was sacrificed to deity. A second reason for torturing and killing cats arose from the "darkness" of feline nature, for occultists aware of the demonic aspect of these animals believed that they were sacrificing a devil to the Devil.

We have seen that the Devil was specially prone to manifest himself as a cat and, consequently, it was assumed to be one of his favourite animals. Cat-familiars, like their owners, served the Devil, and it was believed that cats dedicated to him became more efficient servants when their souls were disburdened of their bodies. So black cats were considered to be acceptable gifts to the Devil, and they were frequently sacrificed to him for purposes of placation.

According to an edition of The *Sunday Express*, published in January 1929, York County in Pennsylvania had been almost completely stripped of black cats. The reason for this was that the countryside had been swept by a terror of witchcraft, and the inhabitants "knew" that a sure way of making peace with Satan was to plunge a live black cat into boiling water, keeping one of its bones as an amulet.

After a Sabbat, newly initiated witches made daily sacrifices to the Devil, perhaps in fear or gratitude, or perhaps just to keep in contact with their new master. Sometimes they sacrificed "bloud of their owne", more often the victim of their devotion was a cat. Isobel Young, a witch tried in 1629, stated that for forty years she had "been in use to take a quick ox, with a cat, and a good quantity of salt, and to burie the ox and cat quick to the salt in a deep hole as a sacrifice to the devil". When sorcerers were molested by the Devil, they found that the sacrifice of a live cat was often the only way of ridding themselves of his presence.

(Sorcerers sometimes killed their cats not directly for the benefit of the Devil, but in order to execute the evil they wished on others. Usually, live cat-familiars were used for this purpose, but there were occasions when a dead cat was more useful to the sorcerer than a live one. We are told, for instance, that the "Dead Man's Candle" was made

> . . . with the grease and the fat
> of a black Tom-Cat.

Such a candle, the wick of which consisted of a dead man's hair, was placed between the fingers of a "Hand of Glory" – the right hand of an executed murderer severed from the wrist during an eclipse of the moon. This candle, it was believed, had the power of paralysing the faculties of anyone on whom its light fell.)

There was a cat-ritual, known as the Taigheirm, practised in parts of Scotland till the end of the eighteenth century, which must have been one of the most atrocious ceremonies in which animals have ever been used.

We already know that cats were believed to have second sight, a reputation arising from their ability to see in the dark. (In Scotland it was believed by many people that cats could also acquire second sight "artificially", by tearing out and eating the eyeballs of corpses. After such an incident, the first person over whom the cat jumped would be struck with blindness. So any cat that entered a room with a corpse had to be destroyed in order to avoid this danger, as well as that of vampirism.) Scots highly valued second sight, and some who were born without it were determined to obtain it for themselves. It was because it was believed that this faculty could be wrested from feline nature by the mass torture and sacrifice of cats, that the Taigheirm came into being.

The massacre of the cats that took place at this ceremony has been interpreted by some people as a means of contacting the Devil, and of bargaining with him for the gift of second sight. But it seems more likely, from the torture inflicted on the animals, that the participants in the rite were more concerned (as are all black magicians) with forcing supernatural entities to submit to human desires. In the Scottish Highlands and islands off the coast, subterranean deities were known as the Black-Cat Spirits, and it was these powers that were invoked in the celebration of the Taigheirm.

The word "Taigheirm" has a double meaning for, according to the way it is pronounced, it means either "an armoury" or "the cry of cats". The two meanings are closely associated, since the shrieks of tortured cats were virtually the weapons used to overcome the resistance that the spirits offered to human demands.

Those who participated in the Taigheirm wore black clothes; the cats that were sacrificed had to be black, and the rite commenced in the darkness of midnight between a Friday and a Saturday. The ceremony lasted four days and nights, during which period the operator fasted.

The cats were first dedicated to the Devil, and, since anguish

was supposed to put them in a magico-sympathetic condition, they all had to be slowly tortured. Each cat would be
put on a spit and roasted before a slow fire. The moment its
pathetic howling ceased in death, another cat immediately
took its place, for it was essential, in this effort to control hell,
that there should be no break in continuity.

At certain points during the rite, infernal spirits appeared
in feline form. These came in continually increasing numbers,
and their unearthly cries mingled with the shrieks of the
victims of the spit, until finally a cat of monstrous size
would appear, making terrible threats. If the sacrificer was
able to keep the ritual going for even longer than four days
and nights without getting too exhausted, it was worth his
while to do so. When at last the Taigheirm was complete,
the operator demanded from the spirits the reward for his
sacrifice. The gift of second sight was the usual compensation
and when granted was retained by the celebrant till his death.
One Scot who performed the Taigheirm received from the
spirits a small silver shoe, which he was told to put on the foot
of every new-born son in his family. It was predicted that it
would bring fortitude and courage to its wearer whenever
he had to face his enemies. The shoe was applied as directed
for nearly a hundred years, until, in 1746, the family home was
burnt to the ground.

One of the last recorded Taigheirms was held in the middle
of the seventeenth century by two unmarried men, Allan and
Lachlain Maclean, who lived on the island of Mull. The
description of this rite gives us some idea of what an ordeal
it could be for those conducting it.

In the early stages of the ritual, spirits in the shape of black
cats appeared, the first giving the sacrificer a furious look and
naming Lachlain "Injurer of Cats". Allan, who was the chief
celebrant – the incantational and sacrificial priest – warned

Lachlain that, whatever he might see or hear, he must not waver, for the spit must be kept turning, no matter what happened. Later, a cat of monstrous size appeared and set up a frightful howl. It threatened Lachlain that, if he did not stop the torture before the largest of all cat-spirits arrived, he would never see the face of God. Lachlain replied that he had no intention of stopping, even if he was beset by all the devils in hell.

The Macleans continued the sacrifice for four days. At the end of the fourth day, a black cat with eyes of flaming fire appeared, sitting on the end of a beam in the barn roof, and its yowling was heard right across the straits of Mull. Allan, although a strong man both in character and physique, was by that time so mentally and physically exhausted that he just managed to utter the word "prosperity" and then sank into a swoon. Lachlain, the younger of the two, was still self-possessed, and he demanded wealth as well as prosperity. Both of these men received what they had asked for, and both enjoyed second sight for the rest of their lives. Allan is alleged to have said on his death-bed that, if they had been able to hold on a little longer, they would have driven Satan himself from his throne.

Lachlain died before Allan Maclean and it is said that, when Allan's funeral reached the churchyard, people endowed with second sight saw in the distance the ghost of Lachlain standing fully armed at the head of a host of black cats. An effigy of Allan in armour was carved on his tomb, and the people of Mull still show visitors the place where the last Taigheirm was celebrated.

Although on a considerably smaller scale, a rite performed at crossroads had much in common with the Taigheirm. The celebrant went at night to crossroads carrying a large vessel of water. On arrival he made a fire and heated the water till it reached boiling-point, when he dropped a black cat into it. Before long, devils began to appear and begged him to stop boiling the cat, but he would not reply until the chief of the devils appeared. When it came, last of all, and asked the celebrant to stop, he allowed it to take the cat, and in exchange he received whatever he desired.

Cats were further victimized in their use as scapegoats. Having a well-established reputation both for actual and supernatural evil, they were, consequently, often made to carry the burden (and suffer the punishment) of sins which belonged to human beings.

The Sufi parable of "weighing the cat", which was written by a thirteenth-century Persian poet, gives an account of a comparatively innocuous case of an attempt to blame a cat for human misdemeanour. There was once a poor man who had a greedy wife. A guest was expected to dinner one day, which meant that the man had had to work even harder than usual to earn enough money to buy extra meat. When he got home, he found that all the food he had bought had disappeared, and his wife swore that the cat had eaten it. Unfortunately for her, however, her husband knew the exact weight of the meat. So when he put the cat on the scales and found that it weighed considerably less than the food, he knew that the animal was not to blame; for, as he said, "If this is the cat, then where is the meat; or, if this is the meat, then where is the cat?"

In La Fontaine's fable of the "Cat's Paw", the monkey makes the cat do his dirty work for him. A monkey and cat were sitting together by a fire where chestnuts were roasting, and the monkey, who was longing for the chestnuts, persuaded the cat to pull them out for him. Every time the cat put his paw in the grate the fire singed it, and as fast as he drew out the chestnuts the monkey devoured them.

We have already seen that, in ancient Egypt, when a

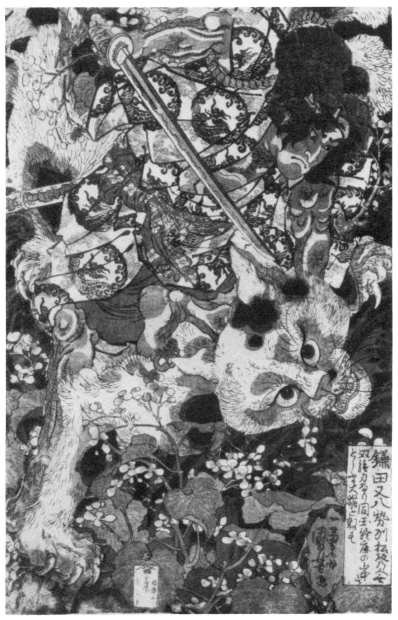

22. Japanese hero killing monster cat *p. 103*

23. Cat-vampire attacking O Toyo *Courtesy Macmillan and Co. p. 108*

woman was drowned as the penalty for adultery, a cat had to lose its life too. There is also on record a case of a French woman who was condemned to death for murder, and was burnt over a slow fire in an iron cage, accompanied by fourteen innocent cats. So it seems that, when a woman committed a crime, the punishment was often divided out between her and a cat as if the animal had somehow participated in the sin.

One of the most blatant examples of a cat's being used as a scapegoat was the Shrovetide custom of whipping a cat to death. This seems to have been an especially popular practice in the Shropshire village of Albrighton. An inn-sign commemorated it with the couplet:

> The finest pastime that is under the sun
> Is whipping the cat at Albrighton.

So it was at the season of confession and absolution of human sin that it was customary to beat a cat to death. Similarly, it is not so many years ago that, on every second Wednesday in Lent, Flemish people hurled a cat down from the top of a tower at Ypres. It is said that black cats disappear every Friday, because it reminds them of Good Friday. Presumably this was the day when cats suffered most from Christians' guilty feelings about the Crucifixion.

Although it was all the same to the cat, distinction must be drawn between such ritual murder as occurred in the drownings, whippings and hurlings mentioned above, and the degrading experience in which cats were persecuted as a sport which had no conscious significance whatsoever. At the end of the eighteenth century, it was still a Scottish form of recreation to hang up a cat in a bottle or barrel which was half filled with soot. Horsemen would ride under the vessel and strike the end of it until a hole appeared. The frantic cat would then spring out covered with soot, and this caused great amusement all round. The phrase "not room to swing a cat in" was derived from a similar form of torment, in which a cat would be held by its tail and swung round as a mark for so-called sportsmen.

Finally, in addition to sacrifices made of gods to deity and of devils to the Devil (in both of which cats were used), there were also those that were made of devils to God.

We have seen how black cats were considered at best to be demonic and at worst to be an actual incarnation of the Devil. (If a cat was seen walking over a grave, Christians assumed that the soul of the deceased was in the Devil's clutches.) In the fifteenth century, when fear of witchcraft became a mania, the cat emerged as a symbol of evil. When Pope Innocent VIII finally legalized the persecution of witches, thousands of women were tortured and burnt at the stake simply because it was known that they owned a cat. Vindictiveness became respectable; the massacre of witches and cats was considered to be the casting-out of evil spirits, and orgies of cat-sacrifices were carried out in the name of religion.

In England, at the coronation of Good Queen Bess, a wickerwork dummy of the pope was filled with live cats, carried with mock solemnity through the streets and flung into a huge bonfire. Protestants declared the cats' shrieks to be "the language of the devils within the body of the Holy Father".

A seventeenth-century book called *Twenty Lookes over all the Round-heads in the World*, describes how Papists tortured and killed a cat which they used to represent a Puritan friar in the reign of Queen Mary. The Roundheads were

". . . so odious to the people that, in derision of them, was a Cat taken on a Sabbath day, with her head shorne as a

Fryer's, and the likenesse of a vestment cast over her, with her feet tied together, and a round piece of paper like a singing Cake between them; and thus was she hanged on a gallows in Cheapside, neere to the Crosse, in the Parish of St Mathew. Which Cat being taken down was carried to the Bishop of London, and by him sent to Doctor Pendleton (the preacher at Paul's Cross) commanding it to be shown to the congregation."

In Roman Catholic France, baskets of live cats were annually burnt on St John's Day in hill-top bonfires in the presence of the local mayor. This rite was still practised at the end of the seventeenth century.

A hundred years later, a similar custom was still observed at Metz. This has been described as follows by Moncrif in his *Lettre sur les chats*:

"Every year a festival is held at Metz which is a disgrace to human nature. The city fathers go in solemn process into the main square, where a number of cats are exhibited in a cage. This is hung over a bonfire which is then set alight with great ceremony. When they hear the frightful shrieks of the cats, the people believe that they are once more torturing an old witch who, it is said, once turned herself into a cat when she was about to be burned."

Even as late as the middle of the nineteenth century, this barbaric practice took place in Picardy. At Hirson, on the first Sunday in Lent, they celebrated what was known as the *bihourdi*. Lanterns and torches were carried through the village streets and it has been described how:

". . . at a given signal, the inhabitants each piled their

share of the kindling round a stake set up in the middle of the village, after which they danced round it, the youths firing off their guns while the fiddlers played. On the top of the *bihourdi* there was fastened a cat which ended by falling down into the flames."

It was explained that the essential elements of this rite were a bonfire and a roasted cat.

And thus the vicious circle seems to be complete. We have seen how the blackness of the cat, which we first found coiled in front of the domestic fire, was responsible for its gradually being drawn full circle into the avenging holocaust.

PART III

The Medium

CATS ARE, of course, not all white or black, nor are they wholly good or evil; and, perhaps because the cat is closely associated with powers of both light and darkness, it has sometimes been thought of as forming a bridge between the two. (Such a "bridge-cat" would, if coloured, presumably be a tabby.)

The Bridge

Many bridges are reputed to have been built by the Devil, and the name "Devil's Bridge" is attached to structures found in England, France, Germany, Switzerland and Spain. Sometimes, as in the case of the Pont de Valentré at Cahors in France, the Devil was entirely responsible for the construction. At other times, he intervened when human engineers, who had started building a bridge, came to the end of their resources.

There was, however, a snag in accepting the Devil's help: for he demanded, as the price of his work, the soul of the first creature to cross the newly-built bridge. A trick commonly played on the Devil was to send across a black cat, so that he received, in exchange for the bridge he had built, not a Christian soul but something he already possessed. Plate 29 shows the Celtic bishop, St Cado, holding a crosier and clad

131

in episcopal robes, meeting Satan on a bridge and handing over to him a black cat.

Although, on the whole, the Devil seems to have resigned himself to this compromise, a story is told of a case where he lost his temper. At Beaugency, a town on the River Loire, Satan was so furious when he found he had been fobbed off with a cat, that he tried to kick down the new bridge. He failed, however, and, as he carried off the cat, it tore at his hands and face with its claws. When the Devil could endure the pain no longer, he let the cat go and it took refuge near Sologne. As a result, the locality came to be known as Chaffin (*Chatfin*), and the inhabitants of Beaugency were called "cats".

We have seen that the cat and serpent are symbolically akin, and there is a gnostic belief that it was a cat that originally sat in the Garden of Eden guarding the Tree of Life with its knowledge of good and evil. Certainly the Egyptian solar cat was found "hard by the Persea tree", which was also a Tree of Life and consciousness. An engraving by Dürer shows a cat sitting at the foot of the Hebraic Tree of Life, with its tail curled round Eve's legs as she receives from the serpent the fruit of the knowledge of good and evil. The Flemish painter, Frans Floris, in depicting the Primal Scene, has also placed a cat at the foot of the Tree. So, again, the cat is not identified with either power, but takes its place between the two with *knowledge* of both.

The cat formed a bridge not only between good and evil, but also between interior and exterior life, and between supernatural forces and men. Celts believed that cats were on intimate terms with all inhabitants of the invisible world, and that cats' eyes were the windows of the fairy king's palace. Through them human beings could see in and fairies could see out, and they illumined the fairies' abode with a strange light.

The cat often appears to be meditating. When it adopts a sphinx-like repose, its narrowed eyes give the impression that it is in touch with an inner life. It appears to have been assumed that, like any other medium, the cat was capable of imparting knowledge thus derived, for it was famed for its oracular powers.

Herodotus referred to Bastet as "Mistress of the Oracle". (We know that she was often identified with Udot, the snake-goddess, and one is reminded of the great Delphic Oracle, where serpent-wisdom was received through the medium of a snake-priestess.) Robert Graves, in his book, *The White Goddess*, describes an oracular cave-shrine in Ireland in which, before the coming of St Patrick, a slender black cat reclined on a silver chair and gave vituperative answers to people who tried to deceive it.

There was also a cat-oracle in Burma. Sinh, the golden-eyed cat which, as we have seen, was greatly revered by the priesthood of the Temple of *Lao-Tsun*, had oracular powers. Its master, the high priest of the goddess with sapphire eyes, took no important decisions without first consulting it. Sacred cats were used for divination purposes in Egypt and, when Lapps were in difficulty, it is said that they consulted a black cat which they regarded as an ancestor. The Chinese turned to the cat when they wanted to know the time.

A Russian legend tells of a wise cat which spent its time perched on a golden pillar, singing ballads and telling stories to people who gathered round it. The cat has been associated with the wisest of saints, St Jerome, who was the father of the Western Church. An Italian painting in the National Gallery shows this saint dressed as a cardinal, and writing (presumably translating the Vulgate) in his study with a cat curled up at his side to keep him company.

The power of prophecy has also been attributed to cats,

perhaps because of their sensitivity to changes of atmosphere, and their apparent precognition of death. The Chinese weather-prophet was a "winking cat" (Plate 15), which slept among peonies and winked an eye at the approach of rain.

Mohammed was very fond of cats. While living in Damascus, he had a cat whom he called Muezza and who used to curl up inside the sleeve of his robe. On one occasion when he had to go out, it is said that he cut off his sleeve rather than disturb the cat's sleep. Apparently he was often seen preaching from the highest tower of Mecca, holding the cat in his arms. Mohammedans still treat cats well: the animal beloved by their Prophet is allowed freely to enter mosques, and the killing of cats is illegal.

The mother cat's habit of carrying her young around in the mouth gave rise to the belief that cats give birth through their mouths. In the Greek myth of Galinthias, the servant who was banished to the underworld and transformed into a cat was condemned to give birth to her young this way. Plutarch goes even further, for he maintains that not only does the cat bring forth young through her mouth, but she has previously been impregnated through her ear!

The cat has been honoured as a symbol of the origin of speech, perhaps through its reputation as an oracle and prophet. Egyptian amulets are often inscribed "Speech of Bastet". The speeches made by goddesses were stylized and always took much the same form. Typical were those found on charms such as, for instance, "May Bastet give life and prosperity" or "Health and happiness to so-and-so". Comment has already been made on the power of the word; it was assumed that such utterances had the power actually to create the conditions to which they referred, and great importance was attached to the manner in which magical formulae were spoken.

The Psychopomp

It is said that cats never lose their way, and perhaps this is partly why the cat came to be known as a psychopomp – a messenger who, like the Greek Hermes, leads men into the underworld.

In Finnish folklore, cats are found transporting men from the outer into the inner world. The *Kalevala*, the national epic of the Finns, describes how, one day, a sorcerer entered a house full of men and started to chant his spells. Within a few minutes,

> ". . . the men were thrown into a sledge drawn by a discoloured cat, and the cat in its rapid course, bore them off to the extreme limits of *Pohjola* [the world of darkness and evil spirits] as far as the vast deserts of Lapland, where the horse's footstep no longer resounds, and the mare's foal finds no pasture."

The Egyptian pharaoh, Tutankhamun, was led into the underworld by a black cat. A gold statuette found in his tomb shows him standing on a plinth which rests on the hips and shoulders of his feline steed.

The Malayan Jakurs venerate the cat. Members of this tribe believe that, when they die, they will be led by a cat on their journey through hell to paradise, and that this animal will spray the infernal atmosphere with water, to lower the temperature and make it more bearable for them.

The papyrus of Dirpu was an Egyptian funerary text which contained magical formulae and symbolical representations of myths assembled for the use of priests and priestesses in the after-life. Dirpu was a chantress of Amon-Ra, king of the Theban gods, and the papyrus bearing her name shows nine scenes, the fourth of which depicts the deceased singer being presented by a cat-headed goddess, presumably Bastet, to Osiris, the king of the dead (Plate 30). The chantress, who carries a spindle, has been led past a terror of the underworld in the form of a door-keeper deity with the body of Bes and the head of a jackal, who holds a serpent and two knives. At the feet of Bastet, who is carrying a large ankh, is the monster Ammut, with a knife between its fore-paws. At the Judgement of the Dead, human hearts are weighed in scales, and those found wanting are eaten by Ammut, the "devourer of the dead". Osiris, who waits to receive the chantress, stands majestically holding his crook and flagellum. Above the scene is a looped cobra, and words spoken by Osiris for Dirpu, who is referred to as "the justified one".

Bastet has been known as "the hidden lady of Bubastis", and the images of her which bear the "feather of Maat" point to her partial identification with the goddess of balance and equilibrium. The place of the cat, in so far as it is a medium, lies *between* good and evil, inner and outer life, gods and men – linking and separating the two. If man consults this animal with access to both worlds, and allows it to lead him wherever it will, he may receive knowledge that would otherwise have remained hidden. If he acquires foreknowledge of future delights in store for him, the cat will appear to be an "omen of good luck"; if he receives a presentiment of disaster, he may declare that the prophetic cat was black!

PART IV

The Symbol

When did cats receive their power?

Historically, the cat was first endowed with archetypal power at the time when, in Egypt, it came to be regarded as a sacred animal. An animal's nature is both light and dark, and the cat is, in reality, both affectionate and vicious. Sanctification of the cat meant that it was ritually purified of the dark aspect of its nature; it was recognized as holy (that is as connected with man's spiritual life), and was thenceforth treated with the respect naturally due to such a being.

Then came the point when King Osorkon, of the twenty-second dynasty, placed the white cat in the centre of a magnificent temple and ritually endowed it with supreme power. From then on, the cat was fully acknowledged to be divine, and the eternal and infinite power of the cat-goddess was believed to be that of the sun, moon and earth.

When the Egyptians "enshrined" the cat, they projected their souls into it. (Reference has been made to the belief that cats enshrine the souls of ancestors, and that when people die their souls go into cats.) The Egyptian cat was irradiated by the light that was shed on it by human consciousness.

It was not until the Middle Ages that the cat was endowed with the power of the Devil. Some women, it was said, "have

137

the power to put their souls into black cats". But these women were witches, whose souls were dedicated to the Devil, and it was their projected, unconscious desire for revenge that darkened the reputation of the cat.

During both the ancient and mediaeval periods of cat-worship, the animals were treated with reserve, for they were looked upon as supernatural beings with whose power, whether divine or demonic, it was dangerous to tamper.

The moment in individual lives when the cat first acquires magnetic power is the moment when it first activates the cat-archetype in them. We all have experience of God and of the Devil, but one cannot help wondering why it is that the cat has been chosen, by so many people for so long and in so many different parts of the world, as a receptacle for arche-typal power both in its divine and demonic aspect. Why has a cat, rather than any other animal, become a symbol for psychic power?

The physique and the natural habits of cats do seem specially suited to attract such projections. The functioning of the cat's eyes, its unearthly wailings, the purring contentment with which it suckles its young, and the diabolical cruelty that it exhibits with its prey have a certain archetypal quality about them. Then there is the fact that the cat appears to have powers of extra-sensory perception. Its fur possesses static electricity and occultists claim that its body is highly magnet-ized; it is hypersensitive to changes of atmosphere; it often appears to be clairvoyant and to experience precognition.

It seems possible, however, that the chief power of the cat to stimulate people's imagination, attracting to itself myth, legend, folklore and fairy-tale, lies in its "unknowableness" – that quality it has that defies human understanding. When we describe the cat as "strange", "mysterious", "inscrutable", "uncanny", "aloof", and "indifferent", we are admitting an absence, delineating a void. There is an unknown quantity here with which we cannot make contact, an intangible which we are unable to affect or control. A gap such as this seems almost to have a power of suction, for, like a vacuum, it seeks to fill itself. I believe that the "magnetic" power of this animal is largely due to the "unknowableness" of its nature, the pull it exerts being the hunger of the gap to fill itself with the projections of those susceptible to cats, whether they be of light or dark psychic experience.

The popularity of the cult of Bastet, which far exceeded that of any other Egyptian goddesses, may have been due to the fact that the cat, more than any other animal, had this gap in its "knowableness", which people could fill with all they valued and enjoyed most. Since the cat was domesticated and so part of their daily lives, the Egyptians must have experienced its nature *inwardly* more than that of other animals, and consequently it would have had more psychic significance for them.

What have people believed about cats?

Several different visions of the cat have emerged, which both arose out of, and created, the body of cat-beliefs.

If you lived in Egypt nearly three thousand years ago, you could take a boat up a broad tree-lined river, and make your way to a sun-drenched temple built on an island in the middle of a city. Within the precincts of the temple, you would soon discover a shrine hidden in a grove of tall trees. In the centre of the shrine, there would be revealed an awe-inspiring image of a white cat-deity, its beauty enhanced by the jewels and gold rings with which its worshippers had adorned it. This being would be attended by priests and priestesses, and would probably be surrounded by sacred cats.

If you lived in mediaeval Europe and chose to wend your

way up a mountain-side on a cold and murky night, you might find a large crowd gathered at the top. In their midst would be revealed the Devil himself, probably celebrating a Black Mass. He would appear as a huge, black tom-cat with fiery eyes, and with green sparks emanating from his fur. He would be attended by his priests and priestesses, the sorcerers and witches, many of whom had flown in on their cat-familiars.

Both deities were the objects of worship, sacrifice, ritual, and pilgrimage, and the centres of orgiastic festivals. Those who honoured the white cat celebrated in the light and warmth of the sun, and feasted on wholesome food and wine. The sexual orgies of Bastet were believed to increase the fertility of the crops, the fruits, the animals and the women. Pilgrims to the black cat's orgies, on the other hand, fed on the flesh of hanged men and unbaptized children. They practised, on moonless nights, what were virtually sterility rites. Since they coupled with demons, their sexual licence bore no fruits, and they ritually produced hail, gale and storm, setting out to destroy crops, kill off animals, and render humans sterile and impotent.

As a god, the white tom-cat was the immortal, self-begotten creator. As Ra, he was the solar fire, the source of power, of light, and of all life. As Osiris, he was the impregnator of the earth, and was also the fertilized seed. He was the hero who fought against darkness, chaos and death.

The white cat-goddess was a healer and a nurse. She destroyed poison, counteracted irritation and strengthened people's powers of recuperation. The tail of her animal-incarnation was widely used to cure blindness.

The black witch-cat, on the other hand, poisoned people's minds, infected their bodies with disease, and inflicted both with blindness. The Devil used the tail of his incarnations to bewitch people, and to bind them to his will.

The white cat was a liberator of the oppressed, and a helper of impoverished and under-privileged young men. It used its cunning and resourcefulness to overthrow the powers of darkness, and brought man wealth, power, honour and happiness.

The black cat was an omen of ill-fortune, bringing poverty and frustration in its wake. It oppressed and tortured; it swindled, tricked and lied to the innocent, and was notorious as a traitor and a thief.

The solar cat which was the "light of the world" was to be found at the foot of Christ, while the demonic cat was seated at the foot of Judas Iscariot.

The third, and final, vision of the cat was received by Celts, who, locating a certain cave, entered to find an oracular shrine, occupied by a slender cat reclining on a silver couch. The cat, which was virtually a medium, formed a bridge, or a boundary, between good and evil, and the inner and outer worlds of gods and men. It had access to, and was at home in, both spheres, and had much prophetic wisdom to impart to man. This was the cat that held conflicting values in balance, in awareness of both but itself remaining "other".

Why have they believed these things?

If we examine the extravagant and conflicting things people have believed about cats, we find that most of them have at least a tenuous connexion with the physique and natural habits of the animal. They have, however, become elaborated and stretched far beyond the bounds of credibility.

From the physical fact that the cat's eyes dilate at night and shine in the dark has arisen its reputation as a moon-goddess with control over the tides, weather, vegetation and human beings. The fact that cats are predatory animals has given rise to the image of a demonic feline monster that emands human sacrifice and lays waste the countryside. The partial has been extended to the absolute: the hardy animal is thought of as immortal, and it is assumed that its power to protect men against vermin in this world will operate against supernatural evil in the hereafter.

To say, however, that these fantastic things people have believed about cats are entirely untrue is incorrect. Folklore, myth, legend and fairy-tale refer not to outer, but to *inner* conditions on a deep level of human experience. They do not tell of objective, but of psychic, events, and though such beliefs may not be true about the animal, they are certainly accurate in their description of what the cat *meant* to people, and still means to many of us today.

The visions of a shining white cat-goddess, of a fiery-eyed black feline Devil, and an elegant oracular cat do not add to our knowledge of the animal, but they give us vivid glimpses of subjective reality. The main pattern of cat-beliefs and stories would never have survived for so many hundreds of years if there were "nothing in them" – if they were not true on *any* level.

Gods, goddesses, demons, and spirits of all kinds are psychic elements externalized from the deepest layers of the human mind, where we are all very much alike. These primordial images, or archetypes, are manifold in form, timeless and indestructible; they have an absolute purity, freedom and power which exist only in the sphere of inner reality.

So what seems to have happened is that the sight of a cat's eyes gleaming in the darkness has activated in people the inner image of a goddess with the form of a cat and the powers of the moon. Similarly, the sight of a cat tearing a bird to bits has touched off the inner image of the Devil, feline in form and monstrous in its cruelty. When we say that facts have got elaborated and stretched, we mean that people started talking

24. Disenchantment. Prince throwing White Cat's head and tail into the fire *p. 111*

25. The Judas Cat *p. 113*

about "outer" cats but finished by describing the habits of archetypal cat-images.

Many of the practices described point to a confusion of "outer" and "inner" cats. For instance, those Egyptians who worshipped their cats appear to have been confusing the animal with the archetype. Humans have always had experience of deity, and Egyptians endowed the cat with the image of Bastet, the goddess. (This recalls a remark by the nobleman in the fairy-tale "Catskin", that, although the girl was a "cat without, she was queen within".)

The physical tail, fur or blood of a cat was used in attempts to cure people of their illnesses. But it was Bastet, not the household cat, who was the healer. Similarly, in the case of charms used for producing second sight, the second sight was that of the "inner" cat, and it was she who had the capacity to see into, and through, things. (Nevertheless, these charms may sometimes have worked, because, although their use betrayed mental confusion, the "outer" cat may have served to activate that psychic entity of which it was a symbol, and the psychic entity *had* the power of healing and clairvoyance.)

The black cats that were ritually burnt were undoubtedly harmless in themselves, but many people saw them not as animals, but as witches, whom they were naturally anxious to destroy.

The extravagant mourning of the Egyptians for their household cats was quite inappropriate to the loss of a common animal. It would, however, have been entirely suitable if they had been deprived of the cat-goddess, and the lengthy funeral rites were obviously honouring Bastet, the "outer" and "inner" cats having become confused. The death of a cat must have been a painful and disillusioning experience for those who believed it to be divine and, rather than face the fact of the animal's mortality, the Egyptians did everything they could to make it live for ever. They did not recognize that it was not a goddess but a symbol of deity, and, rather than withdraw their projections from the animal, they sought to endow it with the immortality of the goddess who they appear to have deceived themselves into believing it to be.

So the study of all that people have believed about cats has much to reveal of the nature of the cat-archetype, and of what it means to many of us. Human beings partake of cat-nature; as we have seen, the cat-goddess is depicted with a human body, and the cats of satirical papyri displayed human weaknesses and vices. The unwinking gaze of a cat is often disturbing, because we feel that it penetrates us deeply, perhaps even "sees through" us. (In fact, what probably happens is that, when the animal stares at us, it activates our *self*-examination, which is carried out by Bastet, operating in us as goddess of truth.) The Celts turned it round the other way by saying that, if you gazed into the cat's eyes, you could see all that went on in the spirit-world. Sometimes the Egyptian "sacred eye" had cats in it, and sometimes the cat-amulets had the utchat engraved on them. It does not matter which way we express it – we may see the cat in us or ourselves in the cat!

How does the cat-archetype operate in us?

Those of us who find ourselves fascinated or repelled by cats have, like ancient Egyptians and mediaeval Europeans, unconsciously chosen the cat as a receptacle of archetypal power. For such people, many psychic experiences are naturally expressed in terms of cat-nature and feline activity.

(i) *Cats' eyes*

The archetypal white cat is all-seeing, and its power flows mostly through its sacred eyes. The sunbeams that pour through the cat-goddess's right eye endow us with health and happiness. They light up the "outer" world, bringing us *fore*sight, and directing our attention to things which, without her, we might have missed. The power of her eye is talismanic, for, by throwing light on our relationships with people and with the circumstances of our "outer" lives, she protects us from the ill-will of others, from at least unforeseen catastrophe, and from accidents precipitated by ourselves.

It is as if moon-beams stream through the left eye of the white cat illuminating our "inner" situation; and it is the archetypal cat's vigilance that, in so far as it operates, prevents our falling victim to unconscious forces of destruction.

The "sight" of the cat's moon-eye is experienced as *in*-sight, and it not only penetrates and disperses our illusions, but also reveals to us the truth. The first human beings may have sprung from the tears of the single eye of an archaic creator-god, but regeneration comes through the eye of the "lunar" cat still operative in our lives. Every time we receive enlightenment – a flash of insight, a momentary recognition of truth – it is the gift of the all-seeing cat whose palace is our centre of illumination. These are our moments of rebirth, the times when the dead parts of us are "revivified", for the shafts of light impregnate our souls, bringing to birth new consciousness.

The archetypal cat knows its way about our inner world, and can direct us to treasures lying hidden in the recesses of our minds, gifts and faculties we did not know we possessed. It is mainly the white cat's habit of illuminating hidden riches that has resulted in the use of its image as a charm. The reason why burying a black cat and closing its eyes with beans is said to ensure that we always have money is that, by killing and blinding the "outer" cat (the recipient of our projections), we increase the capacity of the cat-goddess to throw light on our innate value, of which money is a symbol. In so far as we become aware of our actual or potential talents, we can bring them into play, and like the beckoning cat they will attract, and even create, every kind of good fortune. The fairy-tales indicate very clearly the immense help and riches we can receive through the operation of the "white cat" in our lives.

Finally, whenever we want to learn more about the inner world, the eyes of the white cat are there to be used as windows. According to folklore, we have only to lift up their lids if we want to find out about "ebbs and flows", or to know the time. The rhythm of our inner lives is different from, and often at variance with, that of the outer world; if we get too cut off from our own natural timing, the results are liable to be disastrous. In periods of spiritual aridity, it may be helpful to watch the cat's eyes, for a wink means refreshing rain is on its way.

The eyes of the black-cat-archetype are equally powerful. They blaze with fire which is not of the heavens but of hell; they light up revengeful feelings and destructive intentions, and expose the sterile lust of black magicians. The "evil eye" of the witch-cat can kill with a glance, and it can transform pulsating life into stone. (Our experience of the black-cat-archetype will be examined in detail in a later section.)

There are certain patterns recurring in the ancient stories and beliefs which "strike a chord" when we read them, for they still operate in our lives. The cat-mouse relationship, which according to legend has been there "from the beginning", is a good example, and one worth examining.

(ii) *Cat and mouse*

We all know people who behave like mice, scuttling about, looking grey with fear and feelings of guilt. They are always

half-expecting to be pounced on, and indeed bring it on themselves, for the more they scuttle the more they attract the
notice of potential "devourers". Like the mice described in
the fables, they appear to do everything they can to get
themselves "eaten"! When they are caught, they ignore all
opportunities of escape, appearing to be fascinated by their
torturers. (Where fear and guilt are real they are not, of
course, expressed in this way; it is only when the emotions
are produced by fantasy and false values that people who are
possessed by them tend to behave like mice.) Then there are
the natural "pouncers", who do not especially want to be
aggressive, but feel themselves somehow forced into the role
by the fears and expectations of the "scuttlers". When people
lay themselves wide open to attack it is often difficult not to
meet their "demand" to be wounded.

The "well-established law" referred to by Aesop is a
psychic one. The cat-mouse mechanism operates in, and
through, most of us; but, whereas some people identify more
with the mouse and feel themselves to be perpetual victims,
others live out the "pouncer" aspect of their personalities, for
which they invariably blame their "prey". There are, of
course, people with sadistic tendencies who find the misery of
others satisfying, and those who, conversely, get their satisfaction from being hurt. These mouse-people, in their
determination to be victimized, will even twist harmless
things people say and do so that they appear insulting.
Usually they are not, in fact, being attacked by others, but
by the cat-archetype in themselves, which is for ever pouncing
with demands and criticism.

There is a sense in which the victim and victimizer are
always interdependent, and, while it is comparatively easy for
"pouncers" to realize the absurdity of their feeling persecuted by "scuttlers", it is much more difficult for "mice-

people" to become aware that they are partly responsible for the attacks made on them. Although Cinderella was, like a cat, addicted to the hearth, one sometimes feels that she behaved on the whole more like a mouse. It is not surprising that she was "unwanted", for she was perpetually covering herself with greyness, scuttling about with her endless dreary chores and allowing herself to be "put upon" by long-suffering relatives. The mouse was created, we are told, as a symbol of the sun-god's contempt, and sometimes it seems to represent the deep contempt some people feel for themselves, which is so liable to infect the attitude of others to them. A self-respecting cat would have strolled away and been quite indifferent to the opinions of step-relations.

However much we may desire to succeed in life and to avoid being consumed by pain, sickness and death, there is always a small hidden element in us that wants the worst to happen. In so far as rodents can be said to court disaster, they are symbols of this suicidal entity that is always liable to "rat" on us.

It is extraordinary how many people are revolted by mice. Rodents do not usually revolt children, and they are more disturbing to women than to men. Freudian psychologists maintain that women's fear of mice is of their running up their legs, because the mouse is considered to be a phallic symbol. This does not necessarily mean that such women are afraid of physical sex, for their horror may be entirely of the psychic penetration of which sexual intercourse is a symbol. This does not, however, seem to be the whole answer.

The women who mind mice least are probably those in whom the cat-archetype is most active, for the mouse then appears primarily as that which satisfies hunger. Those most identified with the mouse (usually the more aggressive people, for conscious and unconscious feelings compensate one another) are nauseated because they cannot see one without imagining it mauled, and the sight of these timid, furtive little creatures activates their own neurotic fears and feelings of self-disgust. The only way to reduce the degree of revulsion by mice is to become as aware as possible of all this animal represents to us, and of the extent to which we are identified with the "cat-mouse" mechanism.

Mice are, of course, a perfect menace in our houses, and so, in our lives, are those unintegrated elements of the Unconscious which, when they surface, disturb us and make us restless (the distractions sent by the Devil to St Francis), and, if ignored, may finally overwhelm us.

As legendary mice were always nibbling away at the moon, so are repressed emotions such as fear and guilt for ever diminishing our consciousness. The danger of this "psychic nibbling" and the conflict it produces should not be underrated. It is true that mice are small animals which can gnaw only tiny particles at any one time, but one little hole would have been enough to sink the Ark (containing those elements of consciousness that survived the Flood) had there been no cat around to kill the mouse or frog to fill the hole.

So the value of our psychic cat can scarcely be overrated. It appears to have been created for the express purpose of keeping the problem produced by rodents within controllable limits. (It is interesting to note that, whereas we are irritated by mice, we are scratched by cats. Mice operate very near the surface – scuttling in and out of the skirting-boards – and the wounds of cats are comparatively superficial, for it is the surface of us that they tear to bits. So we are fortunate in that the irritation caused by mice can symbolically be allayed by the scratching cat!) Our danger lies in turning our backs on those unintegrated psychic elements of which mice are symbols. Their "coming to the surface" may bring us restlessness, but at least it gives us a chance to deal with them; and it is "God's cat" in us that attends to these elements and, on our behalf, "assimilates" them.

Rats have always been associated with sinking ships, and if we had no inner cat to protect us from these psychic pests, we would soon drown in the dark and chaotic waters of insanity. It was the cat-moon that hunted and devoured the mice and rats, and our only hope of eliminating corroding guilt, fear and self-contempt is to allow as much light as possible to be thrown on them, so that their nature is revealed and the illusory element dispersed.

(iii) *Cat and snake*

The cat-snake relationship is a far more complex one, for both animals have unusually dark, and exceptionally light, aspects of their nature and associations. Consequently, we find the white cat opposing the black snake, the white cat identified with the white snake, and the black cat identified with the black snake.

The most interesting relationship, and one which we all probably experience, is that of the light cat and the dark snake. Men have always been frightened of snakes, and their very movements can produce a shiver of horror almost as if they were supernatural beings. In a sense, the horror is of the supernatural, for the serpent is a symbol of all that is most dangerous, evil and repellent to us. It was a serpent that brought about the fall of man and continues to be responsible for our general "dis-ease". When this cosmic reptile is reduced to manageable proportions, we experience it as the venomous "snake in the grass", the hidden personal danger that strikes with lightning rapidity. Stealthy, cold-blooded and deadly, it represents a subtle, insinuating evil that

26. Stratagem of Rodilard, the cat *p. 115*

27. Cat and dog fight *p. 120*

28. Rats turning tables on the cat *p. 120*

"wantoneth with the Devil" and works in the dark below
the surface.

Fortunately, the primaeval serpent is not the only power
active in us, for there is also, as we know, the solar cat: we
experience not only disease, but also the healing power of
the cat-goddess. To Bastet, the danger of the snake is *not*
hidden, for she is at home in the world beneath the surface,
and she sees what is going on in the darkness.

She represents our natural recuperative energies which
have the power to fight and overcome whatever is poisoning
us, and the "solar eye", which the cat-goddess personifies,
brings us mental and physical health.

(The destruction of poison and the strengthening of good
health are complementary activities which to some extent
overlap. We take antibiotics to kill our germs, and a tonic
or holiday to "build us up"; psychologists dissolve our
neurotic resistances and at the same time strengthen our
flaccid egos. We saw how impossible it was to draw a clear
line between the functions of the talisman and charm: the
sistrum was used both to fight off dissonant factors and to
strengthen harmony; Dick Whittington's cat both destroyed
vermin and brought him riches. The archetypal cat is a great
giver of life, and every successful battle against destructive
elements puts more vitality at our disposal.)

A great deal of illness is caused by the repression of fear,
guilt, disgust, doubt, and self-deception, all of which are
(as we have seen) symbolized by the rodent and the snake.
Mice are warm-blooded animals which operate fairly near
the surface, and they are primarily objects of irritation and
disgust; but the cold-blooded snake constitutes a threat to
spiritual life, for it represents some deep-seated poison, such
as doubt or self-deception.

The white cat is extremely powerful and it succeeded in

keeping Lucifer out of Paradise; but, if our souls are ever contaminated by the poison from a metaphorical snake-bite, it is a relief to know that Bastet is there to counteract germs of doubt and spiritual death with her fertile seeds of fresh new life. In a sense, most illness is due to unconsciousness, for such emotions, although they may exhaust, do not usually poison us in so far as we are aware of, and admit, them.

Our symptoms are often expressions of those unresolved, inner problems of which we are wholly unconscious. If, for instance, we are unaware of mental anguish, psychic rigidities, or friction, we will probably experience physical pain, stiffness or skin-irritation. If we are unable to swallow and assimilate certain unpleasant facts, we may develop an illness which includes vomiting. Symptoms such as these serve the purpose of relieving the inner stress and preventing our being overwhelmed by it.

Accidents often appear to be ritualistic, an acting out of unconscious psychic events. When an autonomous inner power is mowing down our conscious egos, we happen to get knocked down by a lorry in the street; at a time when we are consumed by an overriding passion, the wind blows a lamp over and the house is set on fire. (If we knock the lamp over or run into the lorry, it is not necessarily a "ritualistic" accident, for it may then be due to an unconscious desire for death.) Sometimes falling ill is nature's way of forcing us to attend to unsatisfactory elements in our lives and "re-form" them. Physical symptoms, and accident-proneness, usually disappear once we have recognized their significance and have come to terms with the psychic situation they represent. So, if we allow the cat-goddess to throw light on our inner patterns, bringing them into consciousness, we may not need to have accidents or develop symptoms; and if we become ill she can heal us by "enlightenment".

The statement that the cat's tail can heal us is symbolically true. When we are ill, we have lost our psychosomatic balance, and the energy normally employed in creative living has been autonomously diverted into creating symptoms. In physical illness, for instance, a great deal of energy is used in creating fever, growths or excreta. In an anxiety neurosis, our imagination works overtime, for we are entirely taken up with producing difficulties and problems and, in particular, fantasies of situations we most dread. The cat's tail is its instrument of balance, and it is the tail of the archetypalcat that has the power to heal us by restoring the equilibrium, so that our creative energies can be more suitably employed.

The extent to which the activities of the cat- and snake-archetypes overlap is extraordinary in view of the overt dissimilarity of the animals. In their light aspect, both cat and snake, when coiled, symbolize eternity; both were used as guardians of temples; both were associated with resurrection (the snake because, when it sloughs its skin, it appears renewed); both have been consulted as oracles, and both had reputations as healers.

In their dark aspect, the cat- and snake-images are again partly identified, for both have been looked upon as incarnations of the Devil; both have been believed to encircle the world, and to fight heroes with fire, waves and venom; both have been associated with the Fall, and have symbolized lust.

The cat has been called a "furry snake". The snake is far more archaic than the cat, and its image operates on a deeper psychic level. Still crawling about on its belly, the snake seems almost to be part of the earth, and it attacks with cold, inhuman venom. The cat, being higher up the evolutionary scale, is nearer to humanity than the snake, and consequently we can relate to it more easily. It is, like ourselves, warm-blooded and suckles its young, and when it attacks it does so with fiery rage. It will be recalled that the cobra that was the eye of the original Egyptian creator-god was later mythologically split up into the solar and lunar cat. The warm-blooded cat, with its unblinking gaze, its hissing and spitting, and its sinuous movements, could indeed be thought of as a more conscious and humanized snake!

(iv) *Cat and kitten*

The expression "I nearly had kittens" betrays an extraordinary identification with the cat-archetype, and a very primitive state of mental confusion!

The mother cat is a symbol of our creativity, and the cat-goddess, operating in the sphere of sensuality, pleasure and contentment, gives us a capacity for deep relaxation and self-abandonment. In orgies such as those of Bast, people give up to pure, irresponsible pleasure, unrestrained and untrammelled by the usual inhibitions by means of which some sort of balance is normally retained. (It is significant that, when the cat-image was used to produce religious music, the rhythms and harmony of the spiritual life, it was on the word "pleasure" that its head was struck.)

Play is at the beginning of all creative activity, for it is only when we can adopt an attitude of purposelessness, and can do things for their own sake, freed of all end-gaining ambition, that something new can emerge which finds expression in sound, words, movement or paint. Through recreation we are re-created, and it is as if we have, like the kitten, to allow ourselves to be picked up and carried by something "other".

Cats are exceptionally good mothers, and it is useful to remember that we have this generous, loving, maternal psychic entity to call on at times when we are feeling particularly bleak and insecure. If Cinderella is thought of as a human girl, it is obvious that all she needed to neutralize the effect of her ill-natured relatives was a fairy godmother (a psychic good-mother); and it is significant that, in several accounts of the story, the generosity and love were supplied by a cat. The fairy godmother of the Perrault version helps Cinderella by showing her how to *use* mice and rats, instead of behaving almost as if she were identified with them. This was one of the factors that transformed the dejected girl into an attractive woman with a cat-like capacity for play. Radiantly happy, the dancing Cinderella soon attracted an eligible prince, whose offer of marriage brought the possibility of her becoming a mother herself.

Dick Whittington was a sort of male Cinderella, for he was a ragged orphan used as a drudge by a bad-tempered old woman. He could not cope either with the irritation of the mice or the irritability of the cook, but "his cat" was able to counteract the bad effects of both. Although Dick Whittington's cat was not exactly a fairy godmother, it was female and its activities released him from persecution and grime, bringing him self-respect, prosperity, a happy marriage and children.

The cat-goddess represents not only the fecundity of nature but, at least potentially, that of human nature, for she personifies the fertile ground of our souls. She protects our psychic pregnancies, presides over our psychic births, and delights in nourishing our psychic children. The fact that the cat-goddess was thought of as virgin indicates awareness that the child she brings us is a spiritual one. She was found in the centre of Bubastis, in the centre of Rome, and in the centre of the family guarding the hearth. She still has her place in the centre of our personalities, where she tends the inner flame which, through her, is continually reborn.

Psychologically speaking, the virgin is someone who is

self-possessed, in the sense that she is never servile to the opinions, wishes or values of other people, nor compulsively attached to their personalities. The virgin cat-archetype symbolizes the uncontaminated soul, the part of us that is unsullied by doubt, and which, when penetrated by beams of light, becomes pregnant and brings forth spiritual fruits. The cat became a symbol of human liberty because the psychic cat is the element of freedom and integrity in our lives.

The black Madonna has been interpreted as a personification of the night-sky out of which the moon is born; she is the ball of dung out of which the solar light emerges, and the unconscious part of our psyches out of which new life comes into being. In fairy-tales, she appears as a dusty virgin of the hearth who is herself reborn as a pure shining beauty. Although the black cat is usually a symbol of the archetype in its destructive aspect, there are exceptions, such as the black cat that heals or the one that brings clairvoyance. In these cases, the darkness of the cat-goddess may be likened to an attitude of *creative unknowing*, in which one waits, in an act of faith, for the light.

The mother cat has, however, her destructive aspect, for she sometimes devours her kittens. It was the dark side of the mother cat-archetype that operated in those black rites when the unbaptized infants of witches were burnt or sacramentally eaten.

(v) *Cat and black magic*

The black cat-archetype is still very active in the lives of many of us, whether operating as a witch, a demon or even as the Devil himself.

According to the mediaeval concept, a witch was a woman who, through making a pact with the Devil, acquired certain supernatural powers. These included the ability to become invisible, to fly, raise storms at sea, produce hail, to evoke evil spirits and to raise the dead. Her most coveted gift from the Devil was the power of revenge, and the witch could kill people by a glance, or transform them into animals or stone. She could blight people's lives in many different ways: by starting epidemics, causing impotence or sterility, and drying up the milk of nursing mothers. As we have seen, she frequently took the form of a black cat.

As a result of her pact with the Devil, the witch was, in the fullest sense of the term, "possessed" by him. Having ritually abused the symbols of her previous religious beliefs, she was baptized by the Devil, branded by him, worshipped him, kissed him on the spot which was the focus of his power, made sacrifices to him and carried out his detailed instructions. Her servitude to the Devil was constantly renewed by sexual intercourse with him; her demonic power was fed by the Black Mass, and by eating unregenerate flesh.

Although we do not know to what extent such descriptions are objectively true, since people believed them it is worth examining their significance. (Orgies such as the Sabbat-meetings have their place in life, but it is naturally located in the unconscious minds of men.) Much that is spoken of as "wickedness" seems to be something that people suffer rather than choose; but an example of evil for which one surely has to take responsibility is that attributed to mediaeval witches. Most of us fight against the activity of the Devil, but these women aligned their wills with his and drew on his power, using it as their own. They deliberately substituted the power of darkness for the power of light, and they appear to have made a free and conscious choice to live out the dark side of human nature.

Within the sphere of the Devil, everything was done to

create emotional bondage. The witch-cat and Satan were very closely associated; and, when the Devil, incarnated as a cat, copulated with a witch, it was with the direct intention of binding her to him. The semen he ejected, which was described as being "cold as ice", reminds one of the hail ritually produced at the Sabbats, and may also be equated with the venom of the cold-blooded snake. The Devil's semen generates hate instead of love; it recreates darkness instead of light and consciousness, and it is a poison which contaminates the soul. The "cold penis" produces frigidity in women, and something like "sex with a cold heart" must be the "abuse" that ties some women, making them "subject and loyal to a man".

Similarly, the witch set out to create interdependence between herself and her cat-familiar so that neither was complete without the other – an example of the way in which a vicious circle is set into being. The black magicians who ate the ashes of sacrificed infants did so with the intention of making it impossible to abandon their heresies.

The shrieks of the cats burnt in a wicker-dummy of the pope were spoken of as "the language of the devils", and we are told that witch-cats talked with human voices, but in an unknown language. The demonic language of these women who were living out their cat-nature was undoubtedly that of the Unconscious, and it would appear to others as a "confusion of tongues".

Many of the powers attributed to mediaeval witches were undoubtedly due to confusion between inner and outer experience. As we know, white cats attracted projections of the cat-goddess; black cats projections of the Devil, – and many of these women, however unpleasant they were, must have received their supernatural powers from the unconscious minds of their contemporaries.

29. St Cado giving Devil a cat in exchange for bridge *p. 131*

30. Cat-goddess leading soul of dead singer through the underworld *p. 136*

All that we have learnt about witch-cats has its place in our own psychic lives. It is important to remember that the witch was a priestess of the moon-goddess, who had been banished by society, and the power that had once made the earth fruitful was switched over to sterilization and destruction. Psychic forces that work against our wishes are always those that we have banished from consciousness, and the witch's obsession with revenge must be the result of this expression of our contempt for her.

The Devil may be thought of as a personification of collective evil. Whereas we may experience the cat-goddess as a giver of life and fruitfulness, the Devil represents the will to self-destruction that fights against our creativity and often sterilizes it. The witch that haunts our inner lives, since she is half human and half demonic, is the embodiment of more personal wickedness. She personifies the "shadow side" of our nature which is clearly in league with the Devil. (The Devil's semen has been compared to the poison of the snake; witches are the avenging furies who were snake-demons and vehicles of the devouring earth-goddess. So, to this extent, Devil and witch are identified.) The witch in us placates her cat-familiar, who in its turn carries out her will. The power of the black cat is that of the witch, and the power of the witch is that of the Devil. (When the witch rides on a tom-cat – or a broomstick – to the Sabbats, she is virtually riding on the Devil's phallus, and allowing herself to be "carried by" revenge.)

The relationships between the cat-familiar and the witch, and between the witch and the Devil, have much in common. The cat suckled by the witch (like the infant demon born of black magic) represents in us the dark side of the Divine Child. In suckling it, the witch is feeding and strengthening the worst side of our personalities, for her milk is a poison which nourishes unconsciousness. The cats given to the Swedish children at their initiation into witchcraft were primarily instruments of sacrifice to the Devil. The adult witch, who sometimes sacrifices the cat itself to her Master, ensures, by feeding him with this psychic element, that her own demonic power will be replenished. In so far as the witch and cat are one, they represent the unregenerate part of our lives which is constantly resuscitated by the Devil's food and semen.

The cosmic cat-serpent reputed to encircle the earth, the Chinese cat-dragon, the cat-fish of St Brendan, the cat of Lake Geneva fought by Arthur, and the Celtic Paluc cat – all represent the chaotic waters of unconsciousness and death. Witches, who personify the disruptive power of the Unconscious, swim around waiting to swamp us with tempestuous emotions, so that we flounder and our consciousness gets submerged. We may also be disturbed by the activity of the necromancer, who takes special delight in raising our dead. There are some psychic elements – for instance those deeply wounded in the past – that should be allowed to rest in peace and not be dragged back to life at the will of the witch. Some experience may be in the process of slipping naturally into oblivion when a cat-vampire infects it, falsely reactivating it, so that, instead of leaving us in peace, its restlessness constantly drains us of vitality.

The power of flight is shared by goddesses and witches. When the white cat-goddess is winged, she soars as the rising soul in our moments of poetic inspiration, bringing us brief glimpses of truth. We experience the levitation of the witch as something different, for it expresses fantasy in its negative connotation, and when the witch-part of us gets "carried away" by desire for revenge, her rising is to heights of unreality.

It is said that, once witches have been summoned by the

Devil, nothing can stop their departure; they fly off with the greatest speed, overcoming apparently insurmountable problems. Similar behaviour is described by Herodotus in his account of how cats flung themselves into fires, and attention has been drawn to the speed at which phantom-cats travel. All this is typical of compulsive behaviour in human beings. When we are possessed by an obsessive idea, we often do acquire almost supernatural strength, and virtually "take off", largely ignoring time and space. At such times, we must surely be "taken over" by the witch-cat archetype operating in and through us, for the strength and speed are not those of a human being with a desire, but rather of the desire itself of which the black cat is a symbol.

There is a sense in which the black cat that "foretells" death *is* death, and the destructive power that flows through the evil-eye of the witch can kill our love, creativity and consciousness. Sometimes the glance of the witch in us brings a particular form of spiritual death, that of petrification.

We saw how the cat has been associated with stone: the Paluc cat was born under a black stone; the head of the Druidic cat fought by Cuchulainn had the properties of stone; there were the "Kit's Coty" dolmen, Scottish monoliths known as "cat-stanes", and the "Cat's Cairn", with its stone resembling a witch-cat's claw. The cat's "unfeelingness" may partly be responsible for this association, for it has always been blamed for its aloofness, indifference and ingratitude – the cold-bloodedness no doubt accounting for its part-identification with the snake. The cat's relationship to the witch is, however, much more relevant, for witches are notoriously stony-hearted, and their power of petrification is to be avoided at all costs.

It is easy to be "petrified" by the horror of the witch in us, and, if we allow ourselves to become infected by her grudges, our open, loving responsive hearts can be transformed into closed, hard, indifferent ones that feel heavy as stones. Many of us have a dead, cold, intractable element in us, and this has undoubtedly been created at some point in our lives by the grudge of an avenging witch-cat. The Tokaido witch herself finally became a stone, and the claw of the Waternish witch-cat was petrified, so presumably the power of these witches to petrify others eventually turned back on themselves. A petrified witch is completely harmless, since, once the bewitching hardness of her heart is fully objectified, we recognize it for what it is and are warned by it.

Sometimes the witch-element does not kill us but only transforms us into animals. This means that she deprives us of our power of choice and objectivity, so that we become completely identified with instinctive desires and our behaviour lacks humanity.

It is the witch who brings us periods of spiritual aridity, who annuls and sterilizes us, who makes us sick and impotent, and dries up our "milk of human kindness". Once are in her power, we are in "troubled waters", and may find ourselves plunged into despondency. So long as she makes us joyless, insecure and resentful, we need to "keep ourselves to ourselves" if we are to avoid her ruining our relationships with others.

When we meet other people in the grip of this archetype, we experience through them vestiges of powers attributed to mediaeval witches and sorcerers. Men and women possessed by deep unconscious grudges will try to get others in their power, harming and even psychically destroying them. They may not have the capacity to raise storms at sea, but they "stir up" trouble and create a bad "atmosphere". They do not feed on putrid flesh, but they appear to relish gossip and bad news. Such people raise evil spirits wherever they go, always activating the worst in others and bringing to light skeletons hidden in cupboards. They kill people's love, blight their creative lives, and petrify them, and they make them act against their own feelings and judgement. They infect them with negativity, destroying their confidence in themselves and their joy in life, so that they fail in whatever they do and become ill. Such women often make men impotent; such men make women frigid and sterile, or they dry up the milk of nursing mothers. Then there are, of course, the human "cat-vampires": people who live vicariously on the life-blood of others, about whom more will be said later.

None of this "blown-up cattiness" is as dramatic as it sounds; most people have experienced it directly or indirectly, to a greater or lesser degree. It is the unconsciousness of such grudges that is so pernicious. Overtly wicked people (far more rare), who deliberately set out to dominate and damage others, are comparatively innocuous, for their intention is obvious and their potential victims have a chance of taking precautions to protect themselves. But the destructiveness of witch-possessed men and women is often "invisible", both to themselves and to others. They deceive themselves that they are nice, kind people who do everything for the best; and others, who get infected and find themselves believing it, become confused and very vulnerable to the archetype.

Man and the cat

Whether those of us deeply affected by cats experience the cat-archetype through our pets, through other people or directly in ourselves, it is important that we should know how best to relate to it. Many hints as to the form this relationship should take were given in the rites, cat-legends, folklore, and fairy-tales.

The Egyptians knew that the white cat-deity dwelt in the

centre of their lives. They expressed their fear of it, dependence on it and gratitude for it; and by honouring it, worshipping it, sacrificing to it, and bestowing objects of beauty and magic on it, they fed all that the white cat signified, thus keeping it powerful and active. These people liked always to have the image of the cat-goddess with them, and, by wearing, handling and meditating on its many aspects, their experience of this deity was kept in conscious awareness.

Legends and fairy-tales have made it abundantly clear that, if we want to receive the many gifts which the cat-archetype has to confer, it is incumbent on us to give it due attention. Those farmers who hoped for the gift of a good crop kept Freya's cats well-fed with milk. The master-priest of the Japanese temple, although poverty-stricken, always shared his food with the cat (thus keeping alive and effectual that psychic element that had the power to bring riches and prosperity). In the Danish version of Cinderella, the despised and impoverished girl gave the cat saucers of milk in spite of being thrashed for doing so. The young men of the fairy-tales, who received generous help from cats, invariably showed respect for the animal, treating it well and relating to all that it represented.

If you adjust properly to the archetypal cat you will find that you are enriched; it is not, however, to be bargained with. The Italian woman gave service to the cats of the enchanted palace without any thought of gain: she just saw what was needed and did it. Then the cat gave her alms which was a gift of money, not payment for services. Dick Whittington had to work hard, suffer much and be prepared to lose what little he possessed, before he received, through the agency of "his cat", all the riches, prosperity and honour he desired.

It is the oppressed, impotent and impoverished element of society (and of ourselves) that is helped by the white cat, and this servant of humanity possesses, or has access to, all the missing power and value which can bring freedom.

One absolutely essential element in our relationship to the cat-archetype is faith. The white cat is the psychic entity which "knows the way", and we must trust it implicitly, honouring, obeying and following it wherever it leads us. (In the fairy-tale of the White Cat, the prince got badly scratched for his loss of faith, which was the result of his not having looked deep enough.) So we must be prepared, like Dick Whittington, to take risks; like the master of Puss in Boots, we must obey the cat's instructions "without knowing what would come of it". The White Cat insisted that no questions should be asked, but assured the prince that she "took affectionate interest in all that concerned him". It was, indeed, only because this young man was lost in the dark, and so had to give up controlling his life himself, that the cat was able to help him at all. He gave himself up completely to the "bodiless hands", and to his relationship with the White Cat, leaving the responsibility of task-fulfilment to her. His final ordeal came when he had to take the risk of killing all that he loved and valued most.

When people are psychically impoverished, it is usually because much of the value that belongs to their lives is still in the power of the Unconscious, where it is hidden from them. Puss in Boots helped his master (who trusted him unreservedly) by using his wits to trick the ogre, so that the land, possessions and servants of this personification of darkness were transferred and put at the disposal of the miller's youngest son.

Royalty is one of the gifts which the archetypal cat bestows on "youngest sons". This means that the youth's impotence is replaced by supreme power, and he is able to rule his life instead of being ruled by it.

Beauty is another grace bestowed by the cat. It is, however, important to realize that, in the stories of the White Cat, Cinderella, Dick Whittington, and Puss in Boots, the cats gave the heroes clothes so that the beauty *which they already had* was brought out. The "white" cat is primarily a symbol of consciousness, and it "brings" people beauty, riches, prosperity, independence, and royalty only in the sense that it brings awareness of all these gifts *latent in themselves*. In fairy-stories such as these, we are shown the flowering of the personalities of young people who have been totally unaware of their own potential power and riches, and the cat usually appears as the "impulse" that starts off a train of events bringing greater consciousness.

It is not natural or right for us to worship the archetype of the white cat, but we need to respect its potential importance in our lives, to trust it and allow ourselves constant awareness of its existence. In so far as the white cat is active in us, life goes well: when it beckons, we receive good fortune; when it gives birth, we are creative; when it kills snakes and rodents, we are healthy; when it illuminates the darkness, we are enlightened. Those of us who are especially fond of cats are probably more in touch than others with the white cat-archetype, while those who "adore" cats, in an irrational way, are probably to some extent confusing the animal with the goddess.

Relating to the cat-archetype in its dark aspect is largely a matter of learning how to protect oneself against it; and again, many clues to methods of dealing with this problem are to be found in the legends, folklore and fairy-tales.

The first essential seems to be that we should recognize a demon or witch-cat when we see one. It was because the Swiss fisherman mistook the feline monster for a harmless kitten that he and his family were strangled; and it was because the sons of Paluc showed a similar lack of insight that the Isle of Man was eventually laid waste. The *naming* of the witch-cat rendered it impotent. The power that elements of the Unconscious have over us is largely dependent on their working in the darkness, and of our remaining unaware of their form if not of their existence.

Advice repeatedly given by Aesop and La Fontaine is: "Do not pretend to yourself that the cat will ever cease to evince cat-nature." The cat is naturally a predatory beast, and if you are stupid and unrealistic enough to believe that it is repentant, or that its bad habits are either reformed or dead, you deserve to be devoured by it. (The archetype will always be hungry and seek to satisfy itself, like the eye of the archaic Egyptian creator-god which "could never be fully or permanently appeased".) It is comfortable to dwell exclusively on the "white" aspect of cat-nature, and indeed on all our more pleasant psychic entities, but to allow the dark qualities to sink into unconsciousness is a form of self-indulgence for which we pay very heavily. The dark elements and aspects are just as real as the light, and they strongly object to being ignored.

It is only to the extent that we are unconscious that we are liable to be drained by psychic forces, for we become prey to succubi and blood-sucking ghosts "during sleep". In the legend of the "Vampire-cat of Nabéshima", O Toyo "woke up to" the threat of evil but, unfortunately, was then overcome by it. We saw how the cat-vampire could only cast its spells, and drain the prince of vitality, so long as he was asleep and his guards overcome by drowsiness. If any single person remained conscious during the night, the blood-sucker was rendered impotent.

There are certain people – "human vampires" – whose presence always leaves us drained. They are usually very negative in their attitude to life, and draw on our creative energy to offset their own destructiveness. It is as if, like the Devil's mouse in Noah's Ark, they gnaw a hole so that strength pours out of us and into them, leaving us feeling wan and depleted. This experience can be expressed in two ways. It can be said that such people are possessed by the cat-vampire archetype which, operating through them, seeks to quench its thirst at our expense, or that their cat-vampire infects "dead elements" in us which become blood-suckers, and it is by them that we are drained. The dead parts of our psyches are particularly susceptible to attack by the black cat-archetype, for witches feed on corpses and cat-vampires infect them. It would seem that the only precaution we can take against such disasters is to keep in constant touch with the white cat-goddess, for Bastet has the power to revivify the dead.

Whether we have to deal with the cat-vampire experienced through other people or in ourselves, we can only fight it by becoming as conscious as possible of what it is we have banished from our lives. As far as the "hole bored in us" is concerned, we have "God's cat and frog" to call on to resolve this problem. If, however, we are totally possessed by a vampire, the cure has been shown to lie in dismemberment. This recalls the experience of the Egyptian serpent, Apep, of Osiris and the corn-cat, and of the moon that Set flung into the abyss – which is of the analytical function employed throughout this chapter. In other words, we may have to be prepared for some degree of disintegration for, if things are chopped up into small pieces, they can be carefully examined and, if necessary, "re-formed".

When we are attacked by unconscious psychic elements we should immediately summon the forces of light to our aid, for "fences of prayer and charms", we are told, prevent the entry of witch-cats. Light disperses darkness, and ultimately the solar cat was stronger than Apep. Bastet is always available to protect us and, if her "sacred eye" is pitted against the "evil eye" of the witch, her healing against the cat-demon's bewitching power of the tail, her life-giving ankh against the blood-draining ghost, her creativity against the witch's sterility and destructiveness, the independence, health, potency and happiness she brings against the bondage, disease, impotence and misery with which the cat-Devil endows us – the dark forces will not stand much chance of survival. It is unwise for us to attempt to fight the black cat-archetype alone, for human strength can easily be overcome by the supernatural. It is best to leave it to our gods, angels, heroes and knights, for these psychic entities have the power and are there to help us.

If, however, we feel that the archetype is for ever playing "cat and mouse" with us and that we virtually are living "under the cat's paw", we are probably exaggerating the part it plays in our lives. The oriental belief that, if you are especially afraid of cats, you were a rat in your last life, should be taken seriously, for conditions said to obtain "in previous lives" often exist on an unconscious level now. It may be that we are identifying too much with the psychic rodent, and need to be more objective about the rat as well as the cat.

Another possibility is that we will ourselves become witches, and, in order to avoid this change, we need to be very aware of the temptation it is for us. Everyone must have experienced at some time, and to some degree, a desire for revenge: the moment we are hurt, the primitive part of us wants to hit back. If we "feed" this feeling and allow ourselves to be possessed by the desire, there is considerable satisfaction of a morbid kind to be had by giving full uninhibited vent to it.

We need also to be aware of the result of succumbing to this temptation. If we fly off in dark fantasies, allowing ourselves to be "carried away" by the black cat (the witch's instrument of revenge), and if we suckle, or allow ourselves to be suckled by, demons, such abandonment to the feline Devil brings a compulsive tie to him, and ensures that we will never be free again. Further, although by "rubbing our bodies with black oil and transforming ourselves into black cats" we may escape recognition for some time and avoid taking responsibility for our nefarious deeds, sooner or later we shall find ourselves *consumed* with the heat generated by desire for revenge.

The greatest danger is that we will not merely be attacked by the black cat-archetype, but will be completely taken over by it. We saw how wounds inflicted on cats often appeared on women, the cats and women being recognized as one; but, in cases such as these, the women were witches and had voluntarily assumed cat-form. Usually, when we appear to others as embodied "cattiness" or "witchery", it is far from having been our choice. We have been taken over against our wills by the witch-cat archetype and, like the woman described by Aesop, although outwardly human, now possess – or are possessed by – the nature of a cat.

The fairy-tale of "The White Cat", which tells of a girl who was forced to spend many years in feline form, has comment to make on such "possession". The mourning of this cat-woman was really for her lost humanity. She had originally refused to accept the ugly monkey which the fairies wanted her to marry, and as a punishment was condemned to live as an animal herself. This is typical of the background to archetypal possession, which is nearly always due to a refusal to come to terms with something we find unpleasant.

As humans can be liberated by the image of a cat, so the

cat-possessed girl could be set free by the image of a human. This tale indicates that once we are spellbound – possessed by an animal-archetype – we can only be released if we are prepared to be "chopped up" (like the man possessed by a cat-vampire), and this is done as a sacrificial act by a remaining human element in our lives.

The primitive belief that, if you kill a cat, you will be possessed by it, points again to the same psychic law, because the "outer" and "inner" cat cannot be completely separated. (The law and justice of the cat-goddess did not spring from social morality, but expressed the inner law of cause and effect. It is a psychic fact, for instance, that, if you are for ever repressing irritation and anger, there will come a time when you will "lose your temper", that is you will be possessed by anger.) The treatment recommended is to eat a portion of the cat's flesh – take part of the banished thing back into your life – for only if it is "admitted" will the risk of possession by it diminish.

The psychic cat that is "apathetic", "melancholy", and "forgetful" is obviously one that is in the power of the witch, and if we allow ourselves to be possessed by it we shall probably find that, in some ways, we are not "coming up to scratch"! It appears, however, that such a cat can be released from the witch's spell if we mark its back with the sign of the cross. This would presumably activate the light aspect of its nature, so that it is transformed into the lively, independent cat that was said to have been born in the stable with Christ.

Those whose personalities contain particularly deep "shadows" are most vulnerable to archetypal possession. It was the criminal, we are told, who was most in danger of becoming a vampire; the woman with grudges who became a witch, and the girl with an ugly monkey to contend with who became a cat. It is very difficult, when we are aware of our crimes, our dark hostile feelings and our ugliness, not to reject them wholeheartedly, and even to try to banish them from our lives so that we can pretend they no longer exist. We succeed at our peril, however, for deep repression makes archetypal possession probable if not certain.

Our best means, therefore, of protecting ourselves against the black cat-archetype is, first of all, to acknowledge its existence (whether it manifests itself as a cat, witch, demon or as the Devil). An attitude of vigilance will ensure that we recognize it when we see it (naming it will render it impotent), and we must beware of deceiving ourselves that it has forsaken its predatory nature. Our only real defence against its attack lies in consciousness: awareness of what it is doing and why it is doing it; and we can call on the powers of light to strengthen and protect us. If, however, we feel we live "under the cat's paw", we should make sure that we are not identifying with the psychic rat. We should be aware of the temptation to become witch-cats, and of the dangers that result from succumbing to it. If we wish to avoid archetypal possession, we should never try to banish or destroy un-pleasant psychic entities, but should give them their due and come to terms with them. If we want to set free a psychic-cat from the power of a witch, we can do so by making the sign of the cross on its back. We need to be aware of the special vulnerability of those of us with deep shadows and, by maintaining contact with Bastet, to keep our "deadness" down to a minimum. Once we are "spellbound", or possessed by a cat-vampire, our only hope of liberation lies in our willingness to be "chopped up" – that is to allow temporary disintegration so that we may be "re-formed".

So, those of us who, at best, dislike cats, and, at worst, are *ailurophobic*, are probably particularly susceptible to activation of the black cat-archetype. To experience fear, hate and nausea when we see a black kitten playing with a bird is obviously irrational, but such feelings are quite appropriate to the vision of a monstrous cat-demon whose claws are tearing the flesh of a heroic knight.

On the whole, the cat plays a greater part in the psychology of women than of men. "Cattiness" is predominantly a feminine trait, and there were always many more female than male witches. On the other hand, male heretics worshipped the cat, and many men today "adore" them. Such men are, however, usually artists of some kind – men in whom the feminine and intuitive side of personality is strongly developed. In female psychology, the cat seems primarily to represent something active and purposeful. It was the handsome prince in certain versions of Cinderella, and the steed of witches bound for Sabbat meetings. In the psychology of men, on the other hand, it has a more passive role to play, whether in the form of a princess or a succubus. But the difference is obviously only one of emphasis, for we have also seen how the mother-cat archetype operates in women's lives, and how men have to struggle with raging cat-devils.

One extraordinary aspect of man's relationship to cats is that sooner or later he always sacrifices them, for, whether the animals were regarded as devils or gods, they always ended up in bonfires. (Two cats appear at the foot of the Celtic cross: a creative cat with its kitten and a cat destroying a bird.)

As far as the victimization of black cats is concerned, our material indicates that it is the "rat" in us that turns on the cat. It is interesting to note that, whereas in life we inflict punishment on the cat and use the cat-o'-nine-tails to punish others, in hell we ourselves may expect to receive punishment from "cat-faced governors".

Whether or not cats are in fact clairvoyant, the cat-archetype can endow us with second sight. It was because men believed that black cats exclusively possessed this faculty, and did not realize that they had it as a potential in themselves, that they tortured and burnt the animals to try to wrest it from them. Probably, the horrible rite activated the cat-archetype, and it was this experience that brought the operator awareness of his own capacity for clairvoyance.

Although in the Taigheirm cats were offered to the Devil, in most other cases the sacrifice was made to God. The animal was then made to bear the blame for human beings, for, in destroying cats, people attempted to rid themselves of sin. The animals were burnt because women committed murder or adultery, and because they were owned by old women believed to be witches.

In the different examples of victimization of cats, we find varying degrees of people's awareness of what they were doing. In the Sufi parable, for instance, it was clear that the woman was aware that she was blaming the cat for her own faults. In the case of the Shrovetide rites, where a cat was beaten to death at a time when Christians were most conscious of their own sins, it is not known whether or not they knew they were using the cat as a scapegoat. In the terrible ritual burnings of cats, the animals were made responsible for the evil of the whole society.

In rites such as these, there must always have been a modicum of awareness that the "outer" cat was a symbol of an "inner" one. The black cat-archetype was the psychic power functioning in the women that was actually responsible for their witchcraft and their crimes of theft, adultery and murder; it was the same dark power that perpetrated those sinful deeds attributed to both the pope and the Reformers. It was this great devourer of consciousness, operating through the Pharisees and incarnated in Judas Iscariot, that ultimately was responsible for the Crucifixion. So it was because of people's confusion of "outer" with "inner" cats that the animal was subjected to so much cruelty.

The sacrifice of "white" cats was quite a different experience, the purpose of which seems to have been to bring about rebirth in the human soul. The cat believed to be a seer was killed so that a sick person could be healed by receiving *in*-sight. The invalid had, of course, always possessed this faculty as an unconscious potential but, so long as the cat existed to carry his projection of it, he could not bring it into play in his own life. The corn-cat, a symbol of the earth's fertility, was ritually killed and sacramentally eaten so that all it represented would become part of the farmers' lives.

In so far as the "white" cat was a symbol of light, healing and salvation, it represented much that was later incarnated in Christ, and, like Him, it had to be sacrificed in order to be reborn.

The meaning of cat-sacrifice appears to have been the destruction of human projections on to the animal, whether they were of dark or light psychic experience. These barbaric practices were deplorable, but it was probably only by burning the "scapegoat" that people were able to withdraw their projections, so that animals could be seen as animals, and archetypes, such as the cat-god and the Devil, could return to human psyches where they belonged. It also meant that people began to take responsibility, both for the sins for which they blamed cats and for the virtues for which they worshipped them. Cat-sacrifice was necessary because of abysmal unconsciousness, and it undoubtedly constituted an act of regeneration.

Once we have withdrawn our projections from cats, we have destroyed our undue fascination by them. The power that the cat appeared to have to attract or repel us was clearly the power of the archetype and, with the withdrawal of this "magnet" back into ourselves, we become free. From this standpoint, outside the magnetic field, we can use the power instead of being used by it; and we can watch pyshic circles, such as that of the cat-mouse, cat-witch and witch-Devil, without getting caught up in them. Like the lords and ladies in attendance on the White Cat, once "disenchanted", we can carry our cat-skins over our shoulders for, no longer spellbound by cat-nature, we are free to wear them or slip them off as we choose.

We then find ouselves in the position of the cat which is a "bridge", and has knowledge of good and evil without identifying with either. It holds the balance between the two aspects of the archetype – perhaps with its tail, since this is its instrument of equilibrium. Plutarch expressed this situation in terms of a "human countenance between two cat-like figures", and explained that the changes in the cat's form could be controlled by understanding and wisdom.

From this position we experience the ambivalence of, for instance, the cat's ferocity, realizing that whether it appears "black" or "white" is determined by our attitude to it. If ferocity is used against the enemies of heroes, we attribute it to the white cat; if it is used against the heroes themselves, we think of it as demonic. Similarly, the trickery of the cat appears "white" if used to render the Devil impotent, and "black" if used against our powers of consciousness. If we accept the activity of the psychic cat, it enables us to fulfil expectations, to compare favourably with other people, and, in short, to "come up to scratch"; but if we oppose the cat that emerges, it lacerates us and we are apt to think of it as an incarnation of "Old Scratch", the Devil himself. In actual fact, the cat is amoral, but, in those of us specially susceptible to this animal, it activates and brings us awareness of both our hidden virtues and vices.

It is the cat which sits at the foot of the Tree of Life that can give us this degree of detachment, so that, instead of being captivated by the light or dark side of cats, we can be open to both aspects of their nature. *In so far as we identify with the cat that holds the balance, we will be balanced in our attitude towards cats.*

We have looked through the cat's eyes into the inner world, and discovered a great deal about ourselves, especially about our feelings of reverence and disgust. Once we are really free of the cat's "magnetism", it is useful to know that the "Hidden Lady" remains seated at the boundary between the conscious and unconscious mind (this is indeed what a symbol is), for we may from time to time wish to consult her oracular wisdom.

Although it is important to guard against being "carried" by the cat (like a witch, or like the spellbound man in the Finnish legend), we may occasionally choose to allow ourselves to be led by its image, in faith that it will protect us against the dangers of the Unconscious, and will reveal to us its hidden treasures.

BIBLIOGRAPHY

D'Aulnoy, Countess, *Fairy Tales*, Trans. J. R. Planché, London, 1894.

Ball, K. M., *Decorative Motives of Oriental Art*, London, 1927.

Baring-Gould, S., *Curious Myths of the Middle Ages*, London, 1872.

——, *Old English Fairy Tales*, London, 1895.

Black, W. G., *Folk-Medicine*, London, 1883.

Boguet, H., *An Examen of Witches* (Lyons 1590), Trans. E. A. Ashwin, Ed. Montague Summers, Bungay, 1929.

Bonnet, R. B. C., *Reallexikon der Agyptischen Religionsgeschichte*, Berlin, 1952.

Budge, E. A. Wallis, *The Gods of the Egyptians*, London, 1904.

——, *The Mummy*, Cambridge, 1925.

——, *The Liturgy of Funerary Offerings*, London, 1909.

Cox, M. R., *Cinderella, London*, 1893.

Davies, E., *Mythology and Rites of the British Druids*, London, 1809.

Davis, F. Hadland, *Myths and Legends of Japan*, London, 1920.

Dodds, G., "Symbolism of an Ancient Stone at Kirk-Braddan", *The Gentleman's Magazine and Historical Review*, Vol. II, London, 1866.

Doré, H., *Researches into Chinese Superstitions*, Shanghai, 1922.

Edmunds, W., *Pointers and Clues to Decoration in Chinese and Japanese Art*, London, 1934.

179

Ennemoser, J., *The History of Magic*, Trans. W. Howitt, London, 1854.

Erman, A., *Life in Ancient Egypt*, London, 1894.

Evans, E. P., *Animal Symbolism in Ecclesiastical Architecture*, London, 1896.

Fraser, J. G., *The Golden Bough*, London, 1932, 1933.

Givry, G. de, *Witchcraft, Magic and Alchemy*, London, 1931.

Graves, R., *The White Goddess*, London, 1948.

Gregory, Lady I. A., *Book of Saints and Wonders*, Dundrum, 1906.

Groot, J. M. de, *The Religious System of China*, Leyden, 1892, 1907.

Gubernatis, A. de, *Zoological Mythology*, London, 1872.

Hartland, E. S., *English Fairy and Other Folk Tales*, London, 1890.

Hopkins, E. W., *The Religions of India*, London, 1895.

Howey, W. Oldfield, *The Cat in the Mysteries of Religion and Magic*, London, 1923.

Johnson, W. Branch, *Folktales of Provence*, London, 1927.

King, C. W., *The Gnostics and their Remains*, London, 1887.

Langton, N., "Bast, the Cat Goddess", *The Antiquarian Quarterly*, No. 4, December, 1925.

Langton, N. & B., *The Cat in Ancient Egypt*, Cambridge, 1940.

Leland, C., *Aradia or the Gospel of the Witches*, London, 1887.

Loiseleur, J., *La doctrine secrète des Templiers*, Paris, 1852.

Martin, E. J., *The Trial of the Templars*, Woking, 1928.

Maspero, G., *Guide to the Cairo Museum*, Trans. J. E. & A. A. Quibell, Cairo, 1903.

Mather, C., *The Wonders of the Invisible World*, London, 1862.

Mégnin, P., *Notre ami le chat*, Paris, 1899.

Mellen, I. M., *The Science and Mystery of the Cat*, New York, 1940.

Mitford, A. B., *Tales of Old Japan*, London, 1871.

Moncrif, Paradis de, *Dissertation sur la prééminence des chats*, Paris, 1767.

More, H., *Antidote against Atheism*, London, 1653.

Murray, M., *The Witch Cult in Western Europe*, Oxford, 1921.

Perrault, C., *The Fairy Tales*, Trans. G. Brereton, London, 1957.

Petrie, F., *Objects of Daily Use*, London, 1927.

Petto, S., *A Faithful Narrative*, London, 1652.

Piankoff, A. (Trans.), *Mythological Papyri*, Bollingen Series XL3, New York, 1951.

Pitcairn, R., *Criminal Trials in Scotland*, Edinburgh, 1833.

Repplier, A., *The Fireside Sphinx*, London, 1901.

Robbins, R. Hope, *The Encyclopaedia of Witchcraft and Demonology*, London, 1959.

Saemundr, *Poetic Edda*, Trans. O. Bray, London, 1908.

Scott, N. E., "The Cat of Bastet", *Bulletin of the Metropolitan Museum of Art, New York*, Summer, 1958.

——, "The Metternich Stela", ibid., New Series, Vol. 9, 1950–1.

Seymour, W. W., *The Cross*, London, 1898.

Snorri Sturluson, *Prose Edda*, Trans. A. C. Brodeur, New York, 1929.

Sommer, H. O. (Ed.), *Le Roman de Merlin*, London, 1894.

Stuart, D. M., *A Book of Cats*, London, 1959.

Summers, M., *The History of Witchcraft and Demonology*, London, 1926.

——, *Witchcraft and Black Magic*, London, 1945.

Swire, O. F., *Skye: The Island and its Legends*, Oxford, 1952.

Topsell, E., *The Historie of Foure-Footed Beastes*, London, 1607.

Various folklore journals.

Vechten, C. van, *The Tiger in the House*, London, 1921.

Visser, M. W. de, "The Dog and Cat", *Transactions of the Asiatic Society of Japan*, Vol. 37, 1909.

Waddell, H., *Beasts and Saints*, London, 1934.

Webster, N. H., *Secret Societies and Subversive Movements*, London, 1924.

Wheatley, H. B. (Ed.), *Le Roman de Merlin*, London, 1899.

Wilkinson, J. Gardiner, *Manners and Customs of the Ancient Egyptians*, London, 1842.

——, *The Ancient Egyptians*, London, 1878.

Willoughby-Meade, G., *Chinese Ghouls and Goblins*, London, 1928.

Zakani, Ubayd., *Mūsh u Gurba* (*Rats against Cats*), Trans. mas uud e farzààd, London, 1945.

Index